NEW
ENGLISH
PRAISE

G000060361

NEW
ENGLISH
PRAISE

A Supplement to
The New English Hymnal

Congregational Edition

CANTERBURY
PRESS
Norwich

Canterbury Press Norwich, St Mary's Works,
St Mary's Plain, Norwich NR3 3BH,
a publishing imprint of SCM-Canterbury Press Ltd, a subsidiary of
Hymns Ancient & Modern Ltd, a registered charity.

New English Praise Congregational Edition.
First published August 2006

www.scm-canterburypress.co.uk

British Library Cataloguing in Publication data

A catalogue record for this book is available from the British Library

ISBN 1-85311-730-7 / 978-1-85311-730-5

Music engraving and typesetting by Andrew Parker,
Ferndown, Dorset BH22 8BB, United Kingdom
Printed and bound by Clays Ltd,
Popson Street, Bungay, Suffolk, NR35 1ED

PREFACE

The revision of a hymn book is a major task and one which has not normally been undertaken more frequently than once in every two or three generations. In the case of *The English Hymnal*, whose centenary we celebrate this year, a complete revision of both words and music took place in the early 1980s and led to the publication of *The New English Hymnal* in 1986. That book has been a resounding success, bringing the *English Hymnal* tradition to a far wider variety of parishes, schools and cathedrals than had ever been the case before.

Yet the creative world of hymnody continues to grow and evolve. New tunes are written for familiar words, new words are written to established tunes, totally new hymns are produced, and hymns which had been forgotten or gone out of fashion are revived. In such a world it simply is not possible to wait until the next revision of a hymn book before making some of these hymns more widely available.

In the same way, the liturgical services of the Church of England no longer remain unchanged from generation to generation. The *English Hymnal* was produced as 'a humble companion to the *Book of Common Prayer*' and the *New English Hymnal* complemented the services, calendar and lectionary of the *Alternative Service Book*. The new millennium has brought us to the era of *Common Worship*, in which a single book has become a family of volumes, some of which have yet to be published.

It is in this context that the editors offer *New English Praise*. It is very much a supplement to the *New English Hymnal*, for that collection – and the many items from the original *English Hymnal* it contains – is still widely used and appreciated. It is for this reason that the numbering of the hymns in the present volume begins at 600.

The book follows the same pattern as the *New English Hymnal*. A collection of fifty hymns is followed by a significant selection of liturgical material providing, together with the existing book, a complete companion to the *Common Worship* tradition. We do not supply new material in every section, but only where necessary to supplement that which the *New English Hymnal* already contains.

The hymns fall into a number of categories. Some hymns have long been known to members of other Christian Churches, but have only recently become popular within the Anglican tradition. Others have appeared since the *New English Hymnal* was published and are thus now made available to those churches who adopted that book. Some ought to have appeared in the 1986 edition but, for some reason, were not included, and a very small number of hymns from the 1906 edition which had been omitted in 1986 have been reinstated. In one or two cases this is to provide hymns for days or readings in the *Common Worship* calendar and lectionary which had been absent from the *Alternative Service Book*. Three hymns, already in the *New English Hymnal*, have been reprinted here and supplied with the tunes to which they are frequently sung.

Some hymns make their first appearance in any major collection. We have provided recent hymns from the monastic tradition of the Church of England, including two for Lent – a season for which there is often rather scant provision in many hymn collections. We have responded to requests for more hymns for minor saints' days, both for those churches and cathedrals where daily services are sung, and for parishes whose patron saint is not provided for by the hymns for major feasts. We have provided new hymns for a few very specific occasions including one for use 'in time of trouble'. We hope it will help the Church at times when we are asked to pray for victims of anything from a terrorist attack to a tidal wave, and in circumstances in which words often fail us.

The Liturgical Section similarly supplements the one in the *New English Hymnal* so that, taken together, they make provision for what is provided in *Common Worship: Times and Seasons*. Contemporary language versions of traditional language texts for such occasions as Candlemas and Holy Week have been provided. Traditional and modern texts for the sprinkling of the congregation with blessed water are given for use on the feast of the Baptism of Christ, at the Easter Vigil and at other times.

We have added many new responsorial psalms, mainly using *Common Worship* texts, and enlarged the section to include a small number of canticles, including those used at the Easter Vigil, so that a contemporary language provision for that day now complements the traditional language selection in the *New English Hymnal*. Used together with those given in the *New English Hymnal,* these psalms provide a selection large enough to cover the whole of the Church's year. The 'Table of Suggested Psalms for Use at the Eucharist' at the end of the book suggests an appropriate psalm for every Sunday in the *Common Worship* calendar.

In addition, a new 'Table of Suggested Hymns' is provided, in which hymns from both the main book and the present supplement are allocated to appropriate Sundays and feast days.

We have added two more popular settings of the Eucharist to complement the two in the *New English Hymnal*. Once again, one is for the contemporary English texts in *Common Worship* and the other uses the text of the *Book of Common Prayer*, but there is no reason why a congregation should not regularly use all four settings in their worship, whether the rest of the spoken text is 'contemporary' or 'traditional'. The original *English Hymnal* was published for a Church in which a Sung Eucharist was a regular feature of parish worship, and we should like to hope that such a service might be revived in those parishes which have allowed that practice to disappear. The four settings we have provided here and in the main book are either already well known or easy to learn, and will enable a congregation to enjoy a style of music which complements that of metrical hymns. Finally, we have included what we might call a 'composite mass', consisting of parts of the Ordinary, or suggestions for them, from a variety of sources old and new. Parts or all of this 'setting' might be used to introduce a congregation to the practice of singing some of the *Common Worship* texts, or as an alternative to the other settings we have included.

A supplement, inevitably, is a more temporary collection than one which would result from a thorough revision of the complete *New English Hymnal*. We have thus felt able to include one or two items which are popular at the moment, but which may be less so in ten or twenty years' time, and which we would have hesitated to include in a more permanent collection.

As a new century of *English Hymnal* tradition begins, the Editors offer the present volume to those many churches, cathedrals and schools in which ordered worship is valued as a means whereby human beings praise and adore Almighty God. From that first 'landmark' edition in 1906 to this modest supplement a hundred years later, the *English Hymnal* claimed and claims 'to be "a humble companion" to the common prayer and worship of the Church of England'. Indeed, we might add that it has become an integral part of prayer and worship in many churches elsewhere in the Anglican Communion and even beyond it. As the present editors celebrate that tradition with joy and gratitude, we pledge ourselves to its continuance and development in the service of all those who 'worship the Lord in the beauty of holiness'.

ANTHONY CAESAR
MICHAEL FLEMING
GORDON KNIGHTS
SIMON LINDLEY
CHRISTOPHER MOORE
MICHAEL TAVINOR
MARTIN DRAPER (*Chairman*)

Ascension Day 2006

Postscript

In a manner strangely reminiscent of 1906, the death of one of our number occurred prior to publication. It seems appropriate to use words from the Preface to the original edition of the *English Hymnal* to record the fact:

One member of the Committee, the late Mr Michael Fleming, was called to rest shortly after the printing of the book was begun. We therefore dedicate to the memory of our friend the work in which he bore so large a share.

CONTENTS

ACKNOWLEDGEMENTS

The English Hymnal Company and the Publisher thank the owners or controllers of copyright for permission to use the hymns and tunes throughout this collection. Acknowledgements are given on-page with the material. Every effort has been made to trace copyright owners or controllers, to seek permission to use text and music, and to make alterations as necessary. The Publisher apologises to those who have not been traced at the time of going to press, and whose rights have inadvertently not been acknowledged. Any omissions or inaccuracies of permissions or copyright details will be corrected in future printings.

COPYRIGHT

GRANTS

Liberal grants of copies of *New English Praise* are made by the Publisher to help parishes and others in the introduction of the book, or in the renewal of existing supplies. An application form for a grant can be obtained from Canterbury Press Norwich, St Mary's Works, St Mary's Plain, Norwich, Norfolk NR3 3BH. An application form can also be obtained by email from admin@scm-canterburypress.co.uk.

EXPLANATORY NOTES

General guidance on the use of the music and the words will be found in the preliminary material to *The New English Hymnal*.

The hymns are printed in alphabetical order in each of the seasonal sections. 'Amen' is printed only at the end of hymns of which the last verse is in the form of a doxology.

Refrains are printed in *italic*.

The sign * indicates that the verse or verses may be omitted without injury to the sense of the hymn.

The sign † before an author's name indicates a slight alteration to the original text. A double obelus ‡ indicates a more extensive alteration.

The method of singing the Responsorial Psalms is given in the Preface to the Liturgical Section, before item 651.

Note on the music of the Congregational Edition

Although descants are given in this edition, the top line of a small number of verses here provided does not follow the melody of the composer's setting. To enable such music to be sung without a four-part choir, the Congregational Edition provides the tune, rather than the choral soprano part.

The instances concerned are:

646 verse 3: in the SATB version, the arranger disposes the melody of each line over a different vocal part – here only the tune is provided for this verse.

682 verses 1 and 2: the composer set verse 1 for upper, and verse 2 for lower voices in the SATB version.

682 Gloria: as in verse 3 of 646, the choir voice-parts of the original shared the melody – here, only the tune is given.

No adjustment is needed in respect of the Gloria to 688 as the composer follows the theme of the psalm tone in the soprano part of the choir setting.

HYMNS

PART I

THE CHRISTIAN YEAR

600

HIGHWOOD II IO II IO   Richard Runciman Terry 1865–1938

HARK what a sound, and too divine for hearing,
  Stirs on the earth and trembles in the air!
Is it the thunder of the Lord's appearing?
  Is it the music of his people's prayer?

2 Surely he cometh, and a thousand voices
    Shout to the saints, and to the deaf are dumb;
  Surely he cometh, and the earth rejoices,
    Glad in his coming who hath sworn: I come!

3 This hath he done, and shall we not adore him?
    This shall he do, and can we still despair?
  Come, let us quickly fling ourselves before him,
    Cast at his feet the burden of our care.

4 Through life and death, through sorrow and through sinning,
    He shall suffice me, for he hath sufficed:
  Christ is the end, for Christ was the beginning,
    Christ the beginning, for the end is Christ.

FREDERIC W. H. MYERS 1843–1901

600 Music: © Oxford University Press, Great Clarendon Street, Oxford. OX2 6DP. Used by permission.

601

LOURDES 11 11 9 9

French traditional melody
Harmony by Andrew Carter b 1939

A - ve, a - ve, a -ve Ma - ri - a; A - ve, a - ve, a - ve Ma - ri - a.

A MAIDEN most gentle and tender we sing:
Of Mary the Mother of Jesus our King.
  Ave, ave, ave Maria;
  Ave, ave, ave Maria.

2　How blest is the birth of that heavenly Child,
　Who came to redeem us in Mary so mild.

3　The Archangel Gabriel foretold by his call
　The Lord of Creation, and Saviour of all.

*4　Three Kings came to worship with gifts rich and rare
　And marvelled in awe at the Babe in her care.

5　Rejoice and be glad at this *Christmas we pray;
　Sing praise to the Saviour, sing endless *Ave:*

ANDREW CARTER b 1939
from the Latin of the Venerable Bede

* *With the omission of verse 4, this hymn is suitable for Feasts of the*
Blessed Virgin Mary, in which case the word 'feast-day' should be
substituted for 'Christmas' in the first line of verse 5.

602

MARY'S CHILD   436 D   Geoffrey Ainger b 1925

BORN in the night —
Mary's Child,
A long way from your home;
Coming in need,
Mary's Child,
Born in a borrowed room.

2 Clear shining light,
Mary's Child,
Your face lights up our way;
Light of the world,
Mary's Child,
Dawn on our darkened day.

3 Truth of our life,
Mary's Child,
You tell us God is good;
Prove it is true,
Mary's Child,
Go to your cross of wood.

4 Hope of the world,
Mary's Child,
You're coming soon to reign;
King of the earth,
Mary's Child,
Walk in our streets again.

GEOFFREY AINGER b 1925

602 Words: © 1964 Stainer & Bell Ltd, PO Box 110, Victoria House, 23 Gruneisen Road, London N3 1DZ

603

EVERY STAR   87 87 and refrain   Sydney Carter 1915–2004

EVERY star shall sing a carol.
　　Every creature, high or low
Come and praise the King of Heaven
　　By whatever name you know.
　　　God above, Man below,
　　　Holy is the name I know.

2　　When the King of all creation
　　　Had a cradle on the earth,
　　Holy was the human body
　　　Holy was the human birth.

*3　　Who can tell what other cradle
　　　High above the milky way
　　Still may rock the King of Heaven
　　　On another Christmas Day?

*4　　Who can count how many crosses
　　　Still to come or long ago
　　Crucify the King of Heaven?
　　　Holy is the name I know.

*5　　Who can tell what other body
　　　He will hallow for his own?
　　I will praise the son of Mary,
　　　Brother of my blood and bone.

6　　Every star and every planet,
　　　Every creature high and low
　　Come and praise the King of Heaven
　　　By whatever name you know.

SYDNEY CARTER 1915–2004

604

HUMILITY (OXFORD)   77 77 and refrain   John Goss 1800–80

SEE amid the winter's snow,
Born for us on earth below,
See the tender Lamb appears,
Promised from eternal years.
  Hail, thou ever-blessèd morn!
  Hail, redemption's happy dawn!
  Sing through all Jerusalem,
  Christ is born in Bethlehem!

2 Lo, within a manger lies
He who built the starry skies,
He who, throned in height sublime,
Sits amid the cherubim.

*3 Say, ye holy shepherds, say
What your joyful news today;
Wherefore have ye left your sheep
On the lonely mountain steep?

*4 'As we watched at dead of night,
Lo, we saw a wondrous light:
Angels, singing "peace on earth",
Told us of the Saviour's birth.'

5 Sacred Infant, all divine,
What a tender love was thine,
Thus to come from highest bliss
Down to such a world as this!

6 Teach, O teach us, holy child,
By thy face so meek and mild,
Teach us to resemble thee
In thy sweet humility.

7 Virgin mother, Mary blest,
By the joys that fill thy breast,
Pray for us, that we may prove
Worthy of the Saviour's love.

EDWARD CASWALL 1814–78

605

COLLAUDEMUS 87 87 87   Traditional French Carol

Alternative tune TANTUM ERGO 195

Alleluia, dulce carmen

ALLELUYA, song of sweetness,
   Voice of joy that cannot die;
Alleluya is the anthem
   Ever dear to choirs on high:
In the house of God abiding
   Thus they sing eternally.

2   Alleluya thou resoundest,
   True Jerusalem and free;
Alleluya, joyful mother,
   All thy children sing with thee;
But by Babylon's sad waters
   Mourning exiles now are we.

3   Alleluya cannot always
   Be our song while here below;
Alleluya our transgressions
   Make us for awhile forgo;
For the solemn time is coming
   When our tears for sin must flow.

4   Therefore in our hymns we pray thee,
   Grant us, blessèd Trinity,
At the last to keep thine Easter
   In our home beyond the sky,
There to thee for ever singing
   Alleluya joyfully.

Anonymous Latin
Tr JOHN MASON NEALE 1818–66
and Compilers of *Hymns Ancient & Modern,* 1861

606

DAS LEIDEN DES HERRN LM

German traditional melody
Harmony by E. W. Goldsmith 1860–1934

Not too fast

A-men.

Also suitable as an Office Hymn

ENTER our hearts, O holy Lord,
To break the bonds that bind us still;
Speak to us your forgiving word
That we may do your perfect will.

2   Renew in us your Spirit's flame,
Burn every evil thought away;
That we may love your holy name,
And freely run your joyful way.

3   We praise you, Father, for your Son,
And Spirit, all-consuming fire;
Eternal Godhead, Three in One,
Surpassing all that we desire. Amen.

THE ORDER OF THE HOLY PARACLETE, WHITBY

The text was inspired by Eric Milner-White, 1884–1963.

607

MORNING HYMN LM François Hippolyte Barthélémon 1741–1808
altered

WITH joy and by the Spirit led
The Church of Christ seeks desert paths,
All else forgotten, God alone
To worship and to follow there.

2 There silence shall set free the will,
The heart to one desire restore,
There each restraint shall purify
And strengthen those who seek the Lord.

3 There bread from heaven shall sustain
And water from the rock be struck.
There shall his people hear his word,
The living God encounter there.

4 All praise to God who calls his church
To make her exodus from sin,
That tested, fasting and prepared,
She may go up to keep the feast.

SAINT MARY'S ABBEY, WEST MALLING

608

First Tune

OLD KILN   77 77

Anthony Caesar b 1924

Alternative tune SONG 13 382

Second Tune

BOWENS WOOD   77 77

Michael Fleming 1928–2006
Homage to David Evans 1874–1948

Alternative tune SONG 13 382

MORNING glory, starlit sky,
Leaves in springtime, swallows' flight,
Autumn gales, tremendous seas,
Sounds and scents of summer night;

2　Soaring music, tow'ring words,
Art's perfection, scholar's truth,
Joy supreme of human love,
Memory's treasure, grace of youth;

3　Open, Lord, are these, thy gifts,
Gifts of love to mind and sense;
Hidden is love's agony,
Love's endeavour, love's expense.

4　Love that gives, gives ever more,
Gives with zeal, with eager hands,
Spares not, keeps not, all outpours,
Ventures all, its all expends.

5　Drained is love in making full;
Bound in setting others free;
Poor in making many rich;
Weak in giving power to be.

6　Therefore He Who Thee reveals
Hangs, O Father, on that Tree
Helpless; and the nails and thorns
Tell of what Thy love must be.

7　Thou art God;　no monarch Thou,
Thron'd in easy state to reign;
Thou art God, Whose arms of love
Aching, spent, the world sustain.

WILLIAM HUBERT VANSTONE 1923–99

609

THIRD MODE MELODY DCM

Thomas Tallis c 1505–85
rhythm slightly adapted
Edited by Ralph Vaughan Williams 1872–1958

Stately

Original Version (melody in the tenor)

THIRD MODE MELODY DCM

Thomas Tallis c 1505–85
rhythm slightly adapted

WHEN, rising from the bed of death,
　O'erwhelmed with guilt and fear,
I see my Maker face to face,
　O how shall I appear?
If yet, while pardon may be found,
　And mercy may be sought,
My heart with inward horror shrinks,
　And trembles at the thought;

2　When thou, O Lord, shalt stand disclosed
　　In majesty severe,
And sit in judgement on my soul,
　O how shall I appear?
But thou hast told the troubled mind
　Who does her sins lament,
The timely tribute of her tears
　Shall endless woe prevent.

3　Then see the sorrow of my heart,
　　Ere yet it be too late;
And hear my Saviour's dying groans,
　To give those sorrows weight.
For never shall my soul despair
　Her pardon to procure,
Who knows thine only Son has died
　To make her pardon sure.

JOSEPH ADDISON 1672–1719

It is suggested that the Original Version be used for either verse 2 or verse 3.

610

SURREXIT 888 and Alleluyas   Anthony Gregory Murray 1905–92

Al – le – lu – ya, al – le – lu – – ya!

Finita jam sunt prœlia

FINISHED the strife of battle now,
Gloriously crowned the victor's brow!
Hence with sadness, sing with gladness:
Alleluya, alleluya!

2   After the death that him befell,
Jesus Christ has harrowed hell!
Songs of praising we are raising:
Alleluya, alleluya!

3   On the third morning he arose,
Shining with victory o'er his foes;
Earth is singing, heaven is ringing:
Alleluya, alleluya!

4   Jesus has closed hell's brazen door,
Heaven is open evermore!
Our adoring praise outpouring:
Alleluya, alleluya!

5   Lord, by thy wounds we call on thee
So from ill death to set us free,
That our living be thanksgiving:
Alleluya, alleluya!

Symphonia Sirenum Selectarum, Cologne, 1695
Tr JOHN MASON NEALE 1818–66

Another translation of *Finita jam sunt prœlia* is to be found at 119.

611

NAPHILL   77 77 D

Harold Edwin Darke 1888–1976

OUR Lord, his Passion ended
Hath gloriously ascended,
Yet though from him divided,
He leaves us not unguided;
All his benefits to crown
He hath sent his Spirit down,
Burning like a flame of fire
His disciples to inspire.

2   God's Spirit is directing;
No more they sit expecting;
But forth to all the nation
They go with exultation;
That which God in them hath wrought
Fills their life and soul and thought;
So their witness now can do
Work as great in others too.

continued overleaf

611

A - men.

3   The centuries go gliding,
But still we have abiding
With us that Spirit holy
To make us brave and lowly —
Lowly, for we feel our need:
God alone is strong indeed;
Brave, for with the Spirit's aid
We can venture unafraid.

4   O Lord of every nation,
Fill us with inspiration;
We know our own unfitness;
Yet for thee would bear witness.
By the Spirit now we raise
To the heavenly Father praise:
Holy Spirit, Father, Son,
Make us know thee, ever One. Amen.

F. C. BURKITT 1864–1935

612 Words: © Scripture Union, 207-209 Queensway, Bletchley, Milton Keynes, Buckinghamshire. MK2 2EB.
From *Sing to God*

612

SKYE BOAT SONG   86 86 and refrain

Scottish Folk Melody
Arranged by James Whitbourn b 1963

Unison

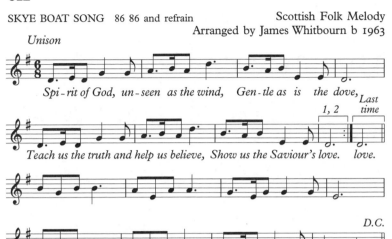

Spi-rit of God, un-seen as the wind, Gen-tle as is   the dove,

Teach us the truth and help us believe, Show us the Saviour's love.   love.

D.C.

SPIRIT of God, unseen as the wind,
Gentle as is the dove,
Teach us the truth and help us believe,
Show us the Saviour's love.

2   You spoke to us, long, long ago,
Gave us the written Word;
We read it still, needing its truth
Through it God's voice is heard.

3   Without your help, we fail our Lord,
We cannot live his way,
We need your power, we need your strength,
Following Christ each day.

†MARGARET V. OLD 1932–2001

613

GUITING POWER   85 85 and refrain   John Barnard b 1948

CHRIST triumphant, ever reigning,
 Saviour, Master, King!
Lord of heaven, our lives sustaining,
 Hear us as we sing:
  Yours the glory and the crown,
  The high renown, the eternal name.

2　Word incarnate, truth revealing,
 　Son of Man on earth!
 Power and majesty concealing
 　By your humble birth:

3　Suffering servant, scorned, ill-treated,
 　Victim crucified!
 Death is through the cross defeated,
 　Sinners justified:

4　Priestly king, enthroned for ever
 　High in heaven above!
 Sin and death and hell shall never
 　Stifle hymns of love:

5　So, our hearts and voices raising
 　Through the ages long,
 Ceaselessly upon you gazing,
 　This shall be our song:

MICHAEL SAWARD b 1932

614

KING DIVINE 77 77 and refrain   Charles Rigby 1901–62

HAIL Redeemer, King divine!
Priest and Lamb, the throne is thine,
King, whose reign shall never cease,
Prince of everlasting peace.
*Angels, saints and nations sing
'Praised be Jesus Christ our King;
Lord of life, earth, sky and sea,
King of love on Calvary.'*

2   King whose name creation thrills,
Rule our minds, our hearts, our wills,
Till in peace each nation rings
With thy praises, King of kings.

3   King most holy, King of truth,
Guide the lowly, guide the youth;
Christ thou King of glory bright
Be to us eternal light.

4   Shepherd-King, o'er mountains steep,
Homeward bring the wandering sheep;
Shelter in one royal fold
States and kingdoms, new and old.

*5   Eucharistic King, what love
Draws thee daily from above.
Clad in signs of bread and wine;
Feed us, lead us, keep us thine.

PATRICK BRENNAN, C.Ss.R.   1877–1952

The inclusion of verse 5 makes this hymn also suitable for Holy Communion.

615

ST WILFRID OF RIPON 11 11 11 5

Christopher Campling b 1925
Harmony by Robert Marsh b 1956

A - men.

CHRIST who has sent us Celtic Saints to lead us,
Faithful and constant, born of contemplation;
Gladly we praise you for all holy people
    Sounding your praises.

2   Forged in the furnace of a burning vision,
Tempered and steeled, through hardships keen enduring;
Swords of the Spirit, may their zeal inspire us
    Driving us onward.

3   Give us the vision of a Church united,
One mighty river, Catholic and Celtic,
Mingle today the stream of living water
    Healing our nation.

4   Father Almighty, Son and Holy Spirit,
Joy of the Saints and of the holy angels,
To you we bring our praise and adoration
    Now and for ever. Amen.

Editors, after a hymn to St Wilfrid
EDWIN LE GRICE 1911–92

616

WORCESTER LM

John Stanley 1713–86
Recast by Michael Fleming 1928–2006

A‑men.

THE Saints who toiled from place to place
Spreading the gospel of God's grace,
Now in their heavenly homeland dwell
With Christ, whom here they served so well.

2 Alert at thy command to go,
And everywhere thy word to sow,
They went, O Master, far and wide,
Eager, but yet unsatisfied.

3 Thine was the task they took in hand,
Thine their good news for every land,
Thine was their power, and thine again
Their passion for the souls of men.

4 That task of thine by them received
To us is given who have believed.
Grant us like them to share thy love
And with them dwell in heaven above.

5 Praise God from whom all blessings flow,
Praise him all creatures here below,
Praise him above, ye heavenly host,
Praise Father, Son, and Holy Ghost. Amen.

vv. 1–3 WALTER HOWARD FRERE 1863–1938
v. 4 after Frere MICHAEL GUDGEON b 1940
v. 5 THOMAS KEN 1637–1711

617

TEWKESBURY ABBEY   76 76 D

Michael Tavinor b 1953

FOR A PATRONAL FESTIVAL

ANOTHER year completed,
  The day comes round once more
Which with our patron's radiance
  Is bright as heretofore.
Now, strong in hope, united
  His festival we greet;
He will present our troubles
  Before the mercy-seat.

2 The Scriptures tell how Moses
    Did for the people pray,
  Appeased the Judge eternal,
    And turned his wrath away;
  Elijah's prayer had power,
    To close and open heaven:
  Such Saints as were aforetime,
    Such Saints to us are given.

3 O Saint of God, belovèd,
    And placed on his right hand,
  Thy prayers be like a rampart
    As 'gainst the foe we stand;
  For Abraham's God is thy God,
    And Isaac's God is thine,
  Thine is the God of Jacob,
    The Lord of power benign.

4 For forty years his Israel
    He fed with Angels' food;
  The flinty rock he opened
    The streams of water flowed.
  Entreat that Christ his people
    May lead to victory:
  The God of Joshua's triumph
    The Lord thy God is he.

ATHELSTAN RILEY 1858–1945
from *Ecce dies nobis* PAULINUS OF NOLA 353–431

PART II

TIMES AND SEASONS

618

DUNEDIN LM

Vernon Griffiths 1894–1985

A - men.

618 Music: © 1971 Faber Music, 3 Queen Square, London WC1N 3AV.
Reproduced from the *New Catholic Hymnal* by permission of the publishers.

THIS is the day the Lord has made
This is the day to celebrate,
The solemn joy of mutual love,
A glimpse of glory from above.

2   Today we make our chief request
That all our homes be richly blessed,
That God may visit every hearth
And stay to guide us on our path.

3   Drive far away the powers of ill
Which poison, separate and kill.
May strategies of Satan cease —
All vanquished by the Prince of Peace.

4   And so together may we be
At every turning glad and free;
Our daily needs by God supplied
With saints and angels at our side.

5   This is the day to praise the Lord:
Creator, Father, loved, adored;
And Jesus, who the victory won;
With Spirit, Power who makes us one. Amen.

BARNEY MILLIGAN b 1928
based on a Collect from
the Office of Compline,
'Visit, we beseech thee'

This hymn is also suitable for marriage services.

619

LORD OF THE YEARS   11 10 11 10

Michael Baughen b 1930
Arranged by David Iliff b 1939

LORD, for the years your love has kept and guided,
  Urged and inspired us, cheered us on our way,
Sought us and saved us, pardoned and provided,
  Lord of the years, we bring our thanks today.

2 Lord, for that word, the word of life which fires us,
    Speaks to our hearts and sets our souls ablaze,
  Teaches and trains, rebukes us and inspires us,
    Lord of the word, receive your people's praise.

3 Lord, for our land, in this our generation,
    Spirits oppressed by pleasure, wealth and care;
  For young and old, for commonwealth and nation,
    Lord of our land, be pleased to hear our prayer.

4 Lord, for our world; when we disown and doubt him,
    Loveless in strength, and comfortless in pain;
  Hungry and helpless, lost indeed without him,
    Lord of the world, we pray that Christ may reign.

5 Lord, for ourselves; in living power remake us,
    Self on the cross and Christ upon the throne;
  Past put behind us, for the future take us,
    Lord of our lives, to live for Christ alone.

TIMOTHY DUDLEY-SMITH b 1926

620

THAXTED   13 13 13 13 13 13

Gustav Holst 1874–1934
Adapted by Compilers of
Hymns Ancient & Modern Revised, 1950

A setting of this tune in a higher key is provided at 645.

Unison

I VOW to thee, my country, all earthly things above,
Entire and whole and perfect, the service of my love:
The love that asks no question, the love that stands the test,
That lays upon the altar the dearest and the best;
The love that never falters, the love that pays the price,
The love that makes undaunted the final sacrifice.

2   And there's another country, I've heard of long ago,
Most dear to them that love her, most great to them that know;
We may not count her armies, we may not see her King;
Her fortress is a faithful heart, her pride is suffering;
And soul by soul and silently her shining bounds increase,
And her ways are ways of gentleness and all her paths are peace.

CECIL ARTHUR SPRING-RICE 1859–1918

621

EAST ACKLAM   84 84 88 84   Francis Jackson b 1917

Alternative setting for verse 3

Verse 3 (organ)   *Unison*

Descant   (small notes)

Most of   all, that love has found us, Thanks   be   to   God.
★ [But to reign in   glo - ry take us   With   thee on high.]

The tune EAST ACKLAM and the harmony to verse 3 was composed to
'God that madest earch and heaven,' 245.

FOR the fruits of his creation,
Thanks be to God;
For his gifts to every nation,
Thanks be to God;
For the ploughing, sowing, reaping,
Silent growth while we are sleeping,
Future needs in earth's safe-keeping,
Thanks be to God.

2 In the just reward of labour,
God's will is done;
In the help we give our neighbour,
God's will is done;
In our world-wide task of caring
For the hungry and despairing,
In the harvests we are sharing,
God's will is done.

3 For the harvests of his Spirit,
Thanks be to God;
For the good we all inherit,
Thanks be to God;
For the wonders that astound us,
For the truths that still confound us,
Most of all that love has found us,
Thanks be to God.

FRED PRATT GREEN 1903–2000

622

TYDI A RODDAIST   86 86 88

Arwel Hughes 1909–88

After v. 3

A - men,

A - men,   A - - - - men,   A - men.

Tydi a roddaist

O LORD, who gave the dawn its glow,
  And charm to close of day,
You made all song and fragrance flow,
  Gave spring its magic sway:
Deliver us, lest none should praise
  For glories that all earth displays.

2 O Lord, who caused the streams to sing,
  Gave joy to forest trees,
You gave a song to lark on wing,
  And chords to gentlest breeze:
Deliver us, lest we should see
  A day without a song set free.

3 O Lord, who heard the lonely tread
  On that strange path of old,
You saw the Son of Man once shed
  His blood from love untold:
Deliver us, lest one age dawn
  Without a cross or crown of thorn. Amen.

T. ROWLAND HUGHES 1903–49
Tr RAYMOND WILLIAMS 1928–90

SACRAMENTS AND OTHER RITES

623

ST BOTOLPH (Slater) CM   Gordon Slater 1896–1979

I COME with joy to meet my Lord,
　　Forgiven, loved and free,
In awe and wonder to recall
　　His life laid down for me.

2　　I come with Christians far and near
　　　　To find, as all are fed,
　　The new community of love
　　　　In Christ's communion bread.

3　　As Christ breaks bread, and bids us share,
　　　　Each proud division ends.
　　The love that made us, makes us one,
　　　　And strangers now are friends.

4　　And thus with joy we meet our Lord,
　　　　His presence, always near,
　　Is in such friendship better known;
　　　　We see and praise him here.

5　　Together met, together bound,
　　　　We'll go our different ways,
　　And as his people in the world
　　　　We'll live and speak his praise.

BRIAN WREN b 1936

623 Words: © 1971 Stainer & Bell Ltd, PO Box 110, Victoria House, 23 Gruneisen Road, London N3 1DZ

624

LITANY TO THE HOLY SPIRIT

Peter Hurford b 1930

Andante e semplice

1 In___ the hour of my dis - tress
2 When___ I lie with-in my bed,
3 When___ the house doth sigh and weep,

When___ temp - ta - tions me op - press,
Sick___ in heart and sick in head,
And___ the world is drowned with sleep,

And___ when I my sins con - fess,
And___ with doubts dis-com - fit - ed,
Yet___ mine eyes the watch do keep:

poco rall.

vv 1, 2

Sweet Spi - rit, com - fort me, com - - fort

a tempo   *rall.*

Last verse

me!   com - - fort me!

IN the hour of my distress
When temptations me oppress,
And when I my sins confess,
   Sweet Spirit, comfort me, comfort me!

2   When I lie within my bed,
Sick in heart and sick in head,
And with doubts discomfited,
   Sweet Spirit, comfort me, comfort me!

3   When the house doth sigh and weep,
And the world is drown'd with sleep,
Yet mine eyes the watch do keep:
   Sweet Spirit, comfort me, comfort me!

ROBERT HERRICK 1591–1674

625

FINLANDIA   10 10 10 10 10 10

Original harmony, adapted from
the symphonic poem *Finlandia* by
Jean Sibelius 1865–1957

Stille, meine Wille; dein Jesus hilft siegen

BE still, my soul: the Lord is on thy side;
   Bear patiently the cross of grief or pain;
Leave to thy God to order and provide;
   In every change he faithful will remain.
Be still, my soul: thy best, thy heavenly Friend
   Through thorny ways leads to a joyful end.

2   Be still, my soul: thy God doth undertake
    To guide the future as he has the past.
Thy hope, thy confidence let nothing shake;
    All now mysterious shall be bright at last.
Be still, my soul: the waves and winds still know
    His voice who ruled them while he dwelt below.

3   Be still, my soul: when dearest friends depart,
    And all is darkened in the vale of tears,
Then shalt thou better know his love, his heart,
    Who comes to soothe thy sorrow and thy fears.
Be still, my soul: thy Jesus can repay,
    From his own fulness, all he takes away.

4   Be still, my soul: the hour is hastening on
    When we shall be for ever with the Lord,
When disappointment, grief and fear are gone,
    Sorrow forgot, love's purest joys restored.
Be still, my soul: when change and tears are past,
    All safe and blessèd we shall meet at last.

KATHARINA AMALIA DOROTHEA VON SCHLEGEL b 1697
Tr JANE LAURIE BORTHWICK 1813–97

PART IV

GENERAL HYMNS

626

AMAZING GRACE CM

Scottish Traditional Melody
Arranged by Robert Ramskill b 1950

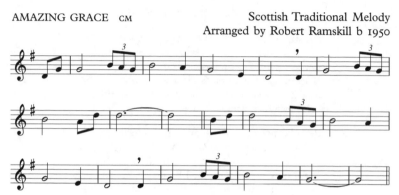

AMAZING grace! — how sweet the sound —
    That saved a wretch like me!
I once was lost, but now am found,
    Was blind, but now I see.

2   'Twas grace that taught my heart to fear
       And grace my fears relieved;
    How precious did that grace appear
       The hour I first believed!

3   Through many dangers, toils, and snares
       I have already come;
    'Tis grace hath brought me safe thus far,
       And grace will lead me home.

4   The Lord has promised good to me,
       His word my hope secures;
    He will my shield and portion be
       As long as life endures.

5   And, when this heart and flesh shall fail
       And mortal life shall cease,
    I shall possess within the veil
       A life of joy and peace.

*6   When we've been there ten thousand years
       Bright shining as the sun,
    We've no less days to sing God's praise
       Than when we first begun.

vv. 1–5 JOHN NEWTON 1725–1807
v. 6 JOHN REES 1828–1900

627

SAGINA   88 88 88 extended   Thomas Campbell, *The Bouquet,* 1825
                                    Harmony from *Primitive Methodist Hymnal,* 1889

Repeat words of lines 5 and 6

AND can it be that I should gain
An interest in the Saviour's blood?
Died he for me, who caused his pain?
For me, who him to death pursued?
    Amazing love! How can it be
    That thou, my God, shouldst die for me?

2   'Tis mystery all: the Immortal dies!
Who can explore his strange design?
In vain the first-born seraph tries
To sound the depths of love divine.
    'Tis mercy all! Let earth adore,
    Let angel minds enquire no more.

3   He left his Father's throne above —
So free, so infinite his grace —
Emptied himself of all but love,
And bled for Adam's helpless race.
    'Tis mercy all, immense and free;
    For, O my God, it found out me!

*4   Long my imprisoned spirit lay
Fast bound in sin and nature's night;
Thine eye diffused a quickening ray —
I woke, the dungeon flamed with light,
    My chains fell off, my heart was free,
    I rose, went forth, and followed thee.

5   No condemnation now I dread;
Jesus, and all in him, is mine!
Alive in him, my living head,
And clothed in righteousness divine,
    Bold I approach the eternal throne,
    And claim the crown, through Christ, my own.

CHARLES WESLEY 1707–88

628

LADYWELL DCM

William Harold Ferguson 1874–1950

Alternative tune KINGSFOLD 376

628 Music: © Oxford University Press, Great Clarendon Street, Oxford. OX2 6DP. Used by permission.

AND didst thou travel light, dear Lord,
Was thine so smooth a road
That thou upon thy shoulders broad
Could hoist our heavy load?
Too frail each other's woes to bear
Without thy help are we;
Can we each other's burdens share
If we not burden thee?

2   O wonder of the world withstood!
That night of prayer and doom
Was not the sunset red with blood,
The dawn pale as a tomb?
In agony and bloody sweat,
In tears of love undried,
O undespairing Lord, and yet
With man identified.

3   As in dark drops the pitting rain
Falls on a dusty street,
So tears shall fall and fall again
To wash thy wounded feet.
But thy quick hands to heal are strong,
O love, thy patients we,
Who sing with joy the pilgrims' song
And walk, dear Lord, with thee.

GEOFFREY DEARMER 1893–1996

629

BE STILL   96 66 66 96

David J. Evans b 1957
Arranged by Martin How b 1931

1 Be still, for the pre-sence of the Lord, the Ho - ly One is here; Come bow be - fore Him now with re - ve - rence and fear. In Him no sin is found, we stand on ho - ly ground; Be still, for the pre-sence of the Lord, the Ho - ly One is here.

Semi-chorus

SATB

2 Be still, for the glo-ry of the Lord is shin-ing all a - round; shin - - ing - round; He burns with_ ho - ly fire, with

with_ splen - - dour crowned.

splen - dour He is crowned.

Descant mf

Unison *Most voices* our

How awe-some is the sight, our rad - iant

rad - iant King of light,_ our rad - iant King!

King of light! Be still, for the glo-ry of the Lord is

shin - ing all a - round.

Semi-chorus p

3 Be still, for the power is

mp

3 Be still, for the power of the Lord is mov-ing in this

mov - ing, to cleanse_

place; He comes to_ cleanse and heal, to

continued overleaf

629

and heal. No work too

mi - ni - ster His grace. No work too

hard for Him; the power of the Lord, the

hard for Him; in faith re - ceive from Him;

power of the Lord. Be

Be still, for the po-wer of the Lord is mov-ing in this

still, be still.

place. Be still, be still.

BE still, for the presence of the Lord, the Holy One, is here;
Come bow before Him now with reverence and fear.
In Him no sin is found, we stand on holy ground;
Be still, for the presence of the Lord, the Holy One, is here.

2   Be still, for the glory of the Lord is shining all around;
He burns with holy fire, with splendour He is crowned.
How awesome is the sight, our radiant King of light!
Be still, for the glory of the Lord is shining all around.

3   Be still, for the power of the Lord is moving in this place;
He comes to cleanse and heal, to minister His grace.
No work too hard for Him, in faith receive from Him;
Be still, for the power of the Lord is moving in this place.

DAVID J. EVANS b 1957
based on Exodus 3. 1–6

630

CLOTH FAIR   86 886   John Scott b 1956

Alternative setting for verse 4

Descant for v. 4

4 Christ be the vi - sion of our lives,_ Of all__ we

think and are; _____ To shine up - on our

spi - rits' sight As light of ev - - er - last - ing

light,_ The bright and morn - ing star._____

CHRIST be the Lord of all our days,
The swiftly-passing years:
   Lord of our unremembered birth,
   Heirs to the brightness of the earth;
Lord of our griefs and fears.

2   Christ be the source of all our deeds,
The life our living shares;
   The fount which flows from worlds above
   To never-failing springs of love;
The ground of all our prayers.

3   Christ be the goal of all our hopes,
The end to whom we come;
   Guide of each pilgrim Christian soul
   Which seeks, as compass seeks the pole,
Our many-mansioned home.

4   Christ be the vision of our lives,
Of all we think and are;
   To shine upon our spirits' sight
   As light of everlasting light,
The bright and morning star.

TIMOTHY DUDLEY-SMITH b 1926

631

RUSTINGTON   87 87 D   Charles Hubert Hastings Parry 1848–1918

A setting of this tune in a higher key is provided at 477

CHRIST the prisoner, Christ the Victim,
    Christ the Judge and Christ the King,
Be with all whom we imprison
    In their pain and suffering.
Let them feel your strength inside them —
    Comfort that shall never cease —
And, to all who serve and guide them,
    Give your healing, give your peace.

2   Jesus, Lord, the thief beside you
    Found that in his dying hour
Casting off his sin and pride, you
    Showed him your forgiving power.
Words of love and hope were spoken
    Words that set the prisoner free.
With the humble, with the broken,
    Lord, we pray, remember me.

3   Poor or prisoner, lonely, ailing,
    Naked, needy, hungry, ill —
Those who visit them and serve them
    Know they do your heavenly will.
Yet more powerful is your teaching —
    We rejoice to find it true —
When with love the lost we're reaching
    Lord, in them we visit you.

4   Father, Son and Holy Spirit,
    Living, loving Trinity,
In the power of Jesus' name, we
    Pray you set your people free —
Free from sin and all that binds us,
    Free to lift your name in praise,
Free from all that gags and blinds us,
    Free to serve you all our days.

KEITH POUND b 1933

This hymn was written for use on Prison Sunday.

632

ORA LABORA 4 10 10 10 4

Thomas Tertius Noble 1867–1953
Descant by Simon Lindley b 1948

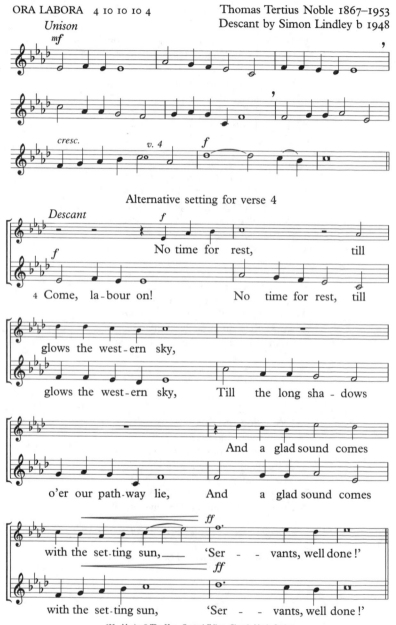

Alternative setting for verse 4

No time for rest, till glows the west-ern sky, And a glad sound comes with the set-ting sun,____ 'Ser - - vants, well done!'

4 Come, la-bour on! No time for rest, till glows the west-ern sky, Till the long sha - dows o'er our path-way lie, And a glad sound comes with the set-ting sun, 'Ser - - vants, well done!'

COME labour on!
Who dares stand idle on the harvest-plain,
While all around him waves the golden grain?
And to each servant doth the Master say,
   'Go, work to-day!'

2   Come, labour on!
Claim the high calling angels cannot share,
To young and old the gospel-gladness bear:
Redeem the time; its hours too swiftly fly;
   The night draws nigh.

3   Come labour on!
Away with gloomy doubt and faithless fear!
No arm so weak but may do service here;
By feeblest agents may our God fulfil
   His righteous will.

4   Come labour on!
No time for rest, till glows the western sky,
Till the long shadows o'er our pathway lie,
And a glad sound comes with the setting sun,
   'Servants, well done!'

JANE LAURIE BORTHWICK 1813–97

633

THE CALL   77 77

Ralph Vaughan Williams 1872–1958
from *Five Mystical Songs*

Come, my Way, my Truth my Life: Such a way as gives us breath; Such a truth as ends all strife: Such a life as kill – – – – eth death. Come, my Light, my Feast, my Strength: Such a light as shows a feast; Such a feast as mends in length; Such a strength as makes his guest. Come, my Joy, my Love, my Heart: Such a joy as none can move;

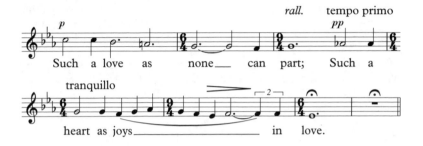

Such a love as none___ can part; Such a
heart as joys_____ in love.

COME, my Way, my Truth, my Life:
Such a way as gives us breath;
Such a truth as ends all strife:
Such a life as killeth death.

2   Come, my Light, my Feast, my Strength:
Such a light as shows a feast;
Such a feast as mends in length;
Such a strength as makes his guest.

3   Come, my Joy, my Love, my Heart:
Such a joy as none can move;
Such a love as none can part:
Such a heart as joys in love.

GEORGE HERBERT 1593–1633

634   First Version

SCHÖNSTER HERR JESU   Irregular   Silesian melody from
                                              Schlesische Volkslieder, Leipzig, 1842
                                              Arranged by Martin How b 1931

1 Fair - est Lord Je - sus, Lord of all cre - a - tion,

Je - sus, of God and— Ma - ry the Son;

Thee will I che - rish, Thee will I hon - our,

O thou my soul's de - light and crown.

2 Fair are the mea - dows,

Fair - er still the wood - lands, Robed in the ver - dure and

bloom of spring. Je - sus is fair - er,

Je - sus is pur - er, He makes the sad - dest

heart to sing.

3 Fair are the flow - ers, Fair-er still the sons of men
In all the fresh - ness of youth ar - rayed;
Yet is their beau - ty Fad - ing and fleet - ing;
My Je - - -
My Je - sus, thine will ne - ver
- sus, will ne - ver fade.
fade, will ne - - ver fade.

JOSEPH AUGUSTUS SEISS 1823–1904
Tr LILIAN SINCLAIR STEVENSON 1870–1960

634   Second Version

SCHÖNSTER HERR JESU   Irregular

Silesian melody from
Schlesische Volkslieder, Leipzig, 1842
Harmony by Martin How b 1931

FAIREST Lord Jesus,
Lord of all creation,
Jesus, of God and Mary the Son;
  Thee will I cherish,
  Thee will I honour,
O thou my soul's delight and crown.

2   Fair are the meadows,
    Fairer still the woodlands,
  Robed in the verdure and bloom of spring.
    Jesus is fairer,
    Jesus is purer,
  He makes the saddest heart to sing.

3   Fair are the flowers,
        Fairer still the sons of men
  In all the freshness of youth arrayed;
        Yet is their beauty
        Fading and fleeting;
  My Jesus, thine will never fade.

4   Fair is the moonlight,
        Fairer still the sunshine,
  Fair is the shimmering, starry sky:
        Jesus shines brighter,
        Jesus shines clearer
  Than all the heavenly host on high.

*5   All rarest beauty
        Heavenly and earthly,
  Wondrously, Jesus, is found in thee;
        None can be nearer,
        Fairer or dearer,
  Than thou, my Saviour, art to me.

6   When I lie dying,
        Still on thee relying,
  Suffer me not from thine arms to fall:
        At my last hour
        Be thou my power,
  For thou, Lord Jesus, art my all.

JOSEPH AUGUSTUS SEISS 1823–1904
Tr LILIAN SINCLAIR STEVENSON 1870–1960

635

ST AELRED 88 83

John Bacchus Dykes 1823–76

FIERCE raged the tempest o'er the deep,
Watch did thine anxious servants keep;
But thou wast wrapped in restful sleep,
    Calm and still.

2   'Save, Lord, we perish!' was their cry,
'O save us in our agony!'
The word above the storm rose high:
    'Peace! be still.'

3   The wild winds hushed; the angry deep
Sank, like a little child, to sleep;
The mighty billows ceased to leap,
    At thy will.

4   So, when our life is clouded o'er,
And storm-winds drift us from the shore,
Say, lest we sink to rise no more:
    'Peace! be still.'

†GODFREY THRING 1823–1903

636

FAITHFULNESS 11 10 11 10 and refrain

W. M. Runyan 1870–1957

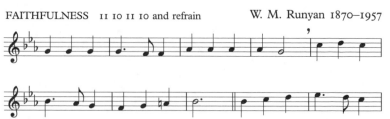

Refrain

Great is thy faith-ful-ness! Great is thy faith-ful-ness!

Morn - ing by morn - ing new mer - cies I see;

All I have need - ed thy hand hath pro - vi - ded —

Great is thy faith - ful-ness, Lord, un - to me!

GREAT is thy faithfulness, O God my Father,
    There is no shadow of turning with thee;
Thou changest not, thy compassions they fail not,
    As thou hast been thou for ever wilt be.
      Great is thy faithfulness!
      Great is thy faithfulness!
      Morning by morning new mercies I see;
      All I have needed thy hand hath provided —
      Great is thy faithfulness, Lord, unto me!

2   Summer and winter, and spring-time and harvest,
      Sun, moon and stars in their courses above,
    Join with all nature in manifold witness
      To thy great faithfulness, mercy, and love.

3   Pardon for sin and a peace that endureth,
      Thine own dear presence to cheer and to guide;
    Strength for today and bright hope for tomorrow,
      Blessings all mine, with ten thousand beside!

THOMAS O. CHISHOLM 1866–1960

636 Words and Music: © 1923, renewed 1951, Hope Publishing Company. Administered by CopyCare Ltd,
PO Box 77, Hailsham, East Sussex, BN27 3EF, United Kingdom. <music@copycare.com> Used by permission.

637

ST BEES 77 77   John Bacchus Dykes 1823–76

HARK, my soul! It is the Lord;
'Tis thy Saviour, hear his word;
Jesus speaks, and speaks to thee:
'Say, poor sinner, lov'st thou me?

2   'I delivered thee when bound,
And, when bleeding, healed thy wound;
Sought thee wandering, set thee right,
Turned thy darkness into light.

3   'Can a woman's tender care
Cease toward the child she bare?
Yes, she may forgetful be,
Yet will I remember thee.

4   'Mine is an unchanging love,
Higher than the heights above,
Deeper than the depths beneath,
Free and faithful, strong as death.

5   'Thou shalt see my glory soon,
When the work of grace is done;
Partner of my throne shalt be;
Say, poor sinner, lov'st thou me?'

6   Lord, it is my chief complaint
That my love is weak and faint;
Yet I love thee, and adore;
O for grace to love thee more!

WILLIAM COWPER 1731–1800

638

PENLAN 76 76 D

David Jenkins 1849–1915

IN heavenly love abiding,
    No change my heart shall fear;
And safe is such confiding,
    For nothing changes here:
The storm may roar without me,
    My heart may low be laid;
But God is round about me,
    And can I be dismayed?

2   Wherever he may guide me,
        No want shall turn me back;
    My shepherd is beside me,
        And nothing can I lack:
    His wisdom ever waketh,
        His sight is never dim;
    He knows the way he taketh,
        And I will walk with him.

3   Green pastures are before me,
        Which yet I have not seen;
    Bright skies will soon be o'er me,
        Where dark the clouds have been:
    My hope I cannot measure,
        My path to life is free;
    My Saviour has my treasure,
        And he will walk with me.

ANNA LAETITIA WARING 1823–1910

639

First Tune

CROFT'S 136TH   66 66 88   Melody by William Croft 1678–1727

A setting of this tune in a lower key is provided at 127.

Second Tune

EASTVIEW   66 66 88   James Vernon Lee 1892–1959

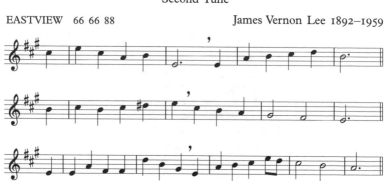

JOIN all the glorious names
Of wisdom, love, and power,
That ever mortals knew,
That angels ever bore:
All are too mean to speak his worth,
Too mean to set my *Saviour* forth.

2   But O what gentle terms,
        What condescending ways
        Doth our *Redeemer* use
        To teach his heavenly grace!
    Mine eyes with joy and wonder see
    What forms of love he bears for me.

3   Great *Prophet* of my God,
        My tongue would bless thy name;
        By thee the joyful news
        Of our salvation came:
    The joyful news of sins forgiven,
    Of hell subdued and peace with heaven.

4   Jesus my great *High-Priest*
        Offered his blood and died;
        My guilty conscience seeks
        No sacrifice beside:
    His powerful blood did once atone,
    And now it pleads before the throne.

5   My dear almighty *Lord,*
        My conqueror and my king,
        Thy sceptre and thy sword,
        Thy reign of grace, I sing;
    Thine is the power: behold I sit
    In willing bonds before thy feet.

6   Now let my soul arise,
        And tread the tempter down;
        My *Captain* leads me forth
        To conquest and a crown.
    A feeble saint shall win the day,
    Though death and hell obstruct the way.

7   Should all the hosts of death,
        And powers of hell unknown,
        Put their most dreadful forms
        Of rage and mischief on,
    I shall be safe, for *Christ* displays
    Superior power, and guardian grace.

ISAAC WATTS 1674–1748

640

LUDGATE   666 D

John Dykes Bower 1905–81

LET every Christian pray,
This day, and every day,
Come, Holy Spirit, come!
Was not the Church we love
Commissioned from above?
Come, Holy Spirit, come!

2   The Spirit brought to birth
The Church of Christ on earth
To seek and save the lost:
Never has he withdrawn,
Since that tremendous dawn,
His gifts at Pentecost.

3   Age after age, he strove
To teach her how to love:
Come, Holy Spirit come!
Age after age, anew,
She proved the gospel true:
Come, Holy Spirit, come!

4   Only the Spirit's power
Can fit us for this hour:
Come, Holy Spirit, come!
Instruct, inspire, unite;
And make us see the light:
Come, Holy Spirit, come!

FRED PRATT GREEN 1903–2000

641

CRUCIFER 10 10 and refrain

Sydney Hugo Nicholson 1875–1947
Descant by Harold Edwin Darke 1888–1976

Unison

Lift high the Cross, the love of Christ pro - claim Till

Fine

all the world____ a - dore____ his sa - cred name.

Harmony

D.C.

Descant

Melody

LIFT high the Cross, the love of Christ proclaim
Till all the world adore his sacred name.

2   Come, let us follow where our Captain trod,
Our King victorious, Christ the Son of God.

*3   Led on their way by this triumphant sign,
The hosts of God in conquering ranks combine.

*4   Each new-born soldier of the Crucified
Bears on his brow the seal of him who died.

*5   This is the sign which Satan's legions fear
And angels veil their faces to revere.

*6   Saved by this Cross whereon their Lord was slain,
The sons of Adam their lost home regain.

*7   From north and south, from east and west they raise
In growing unison their song of praise.

8   O Lord, once lifted on the glorious tree,
As thou hast promised, draw us unto thee.

9   Let every race and every language tell
Of him who saves our souls from death and hell.

10   From farthest regions let them homage bring,
And on his Cross adore their Saviour King.

11   Set up thy throne, that earth's despair may cease
Beneath the shadow of its healing peace.

12   For thy blest Cross which doth for all atone
Creation's praises rise before thy throne.

GEORGE WILLIAM KITCHIN 1827–1912
and ‡MICHAEL ROBERT NEWBOLT 1874–1956

641 Words: Hymns Ancient & Modern Ltd, St Mary's Works, St Mary's Plain, Norwich NR3 3BH

642

UT QUEANT LAXIS   11 11 11 5

Rouen church melody
Harmony by J. H. Arnold 1887–1956

Alternative tune ISTE CONFESSOR 210

A – – – men.

642 Harmonisation: From *The English Hymnal*, 1906, Oxford University Press, Great Clarendon Street, Oxford. OX2 6DP.
Used by permission.

MEN write their verses, night of silence broken,
Words in their order to the one Word spoken,
Sounding with music, making song the token
    Of life eternal.

2   Spirit of Jesus, breathe through all our learning,
Flame of the prophet, wheel of knowledge turning,
Hunger of science, and of art the yearning
    For life eternal.

3   Finger of God, the author of repentance,
Shrinking Belshazzar with the silent sentence,
Casting out evil, pointing to the entrance
    Of life eternal.

4   Praise to the Father, Lord of all creation,
Praise to the Word, whose flesh is our salvation,
Praise to the Spirit of our inspiration
    For life eternal. Amen.

HILARY GREENWOOD, SSM   1929–2003

643

SOMERSTOWN   76 76 D   A. T. Batts 1900–78

NOW, from the heav'ns descending,
　Is seen a glorious light,
The Bride of Christ in splendour,
　Arrayed in purest white.
She is the Holy City,
　Whose radiance is the grace
Of all the saints in glory,
　From every time and place.

2　This is the hour of gladness
　　For Bridegroom and for Bride;
　The Lamb's great feast is ready;
　　His Bride is at his side.
　How bless'd are those invited
　　To share his wedding-feast:
　The least become the greatest,
　　The greatest are the least.

3　He who is throned in heaven
　　Takes up his dwelling-place
　Among his chosen people
　　Who see him face to face.
　No sound is heard of weeping,
　　For pain and sorrow cease,
　And sin shall reign no longer,
　　But love and joy and peace.

4　See how a new creation
　　Is brought at last to birth,
　A new and glorious heaven,
　　A new and glorious earth.
　Death's power for ever broken,
　　Its empire swept away,
　The promised dawn of glory
　　Begins its endless day.

JAMES QUINN b 1919

644

THAXTED   76 76 triple

Gustav Holst 1874–1934
Adapted by Compilers of
Hymns Ancient & Modern Revised, 1950

A setting of this tune in a lower key is provided at 620.

Unison

O GOD beyond all praising,
  We worship you today
And sing the love amazing
  That songs cannot repay;
For we can only wonder
  At every gift you send,
At blessings without number
  And mercies without end:
We lift our hearts before you
  And wait upon your word,
We honour and adore you,
  Our great and mighty Lord.

2   Then hear, O gracious Saviour,
  Accept the love we bring,
That we who know your favour
  May serve you as our king;
And whether our tomorrows
  Be filled with good or ill,
We'll triumph through our sorrows
  And rise to bless you still:
To marvel at your beauty
  And glory in your ways,
And make a joyful duty
  Our sacrifice of praise.

MICHAEL PERRY 1942–96

645

AUCTORITATE SAECULI   LM

Angers Church Melody
Harmony by J. H. Arnold 1887–1956

A   –   –   –   men.

Also suitable as an Office Hymn, especially at midday or on Saturday.

THE breath of God, which ev'ry heart
Inspires with prophecy and art,
Moves mother Mary to conceive
The word prophetic hearts believe.

2   God lifts a curtain, making Man
The actor of his saving plan;
And he whose speech can rouse the dead
Is cradled in the House of Bread.

3   Praise to the Father of the Earth,
Praise to the Son of twofold birth,
Praise to the Spirit, by whose light
The truth in flesh turns wrong to right.   Amen.

HILARY GREENWOOD, SSM   1929–2003

645   Harmonisation: From *The English Hymnal,* 1906, Oxford University Press, Great Clarendon Street, Oxford.   OX2 6DP.
Used by permission.
645   Words: © The Society of the Sacred Mission, 30 Bourne Street, London SW1W 8JJ. Used by permission.

646

ENGELBERG 10 10 10 and Alleluya   Charles Villiers Stanford 1852–1924
                                          Arranged by John Wilson 1905–92

With breadth (♩ = 88)

Unison

1 When, in our mu-sic, God is glo-ri-fied,___ And a-do-
2 How of-ten, mak-ing mu-sic, we have found___ A new di-

-ra-tion leaves no room for pride,___ It is as though the whole cre-
-men-sion in the world of sound,___ As wor-ship moved us to a

-a-tion cried:___ Al - - le - lu - - ya!
more pro-found___

Harmony
mf

3 So has the Church, in li-tur-gy and song,___ In faith and

cresc.

love, through cen-tu-ries of wrong, Borne wit-ness to the truth in

ev - ery tongue:___ Al - - le - lu - - ya!

Upper voices (v. 4 may be omitted)
mp

4 And did not Je-sus sing a Psalm that night___ When ut-most

continued overleaf

646

646 Words: © 1972 Stainer & Bell Ltd, PO Box 110, Victoria House, 23 Gruneisen Road, London N3 1DZ

WHEN, in our music, God is glorified,
And adoration leaves no room for pride,
It is as though the whole creation cried:
   Alleluya!

2   How often, making music, we have found
A new dimension in the world of sound,
As worship moved us to a more profound
   Alleluya!

3   So has the Church, in liturgy and song,
In faith and love, through centuries of wrong,
Borne witness to the truth in every tongue:
   Alleluya!

*4   And did not Jesus sing a Psalm that night
When utmost evil strove against the Light?
Then let us sing, for whom he won the fight:
   Alleluya!

5   Let every instrument be tuned for praise!
Let all rejoice who have a voice to raise!
And may God give us faith to sing always:
   Alleluya!

FRED PRATT GREEN 1903–2000

Verse 4 is probably best used only on Maundy Thursday or at Corpus Christi.

647

KELVINGROVE   76 76 77 76

Scottish Traditional Melody
Arranged by Lionel Dakers 1924–2003

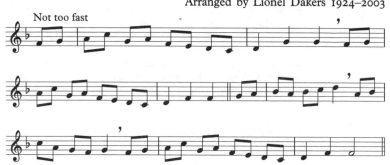

WILL you come and follow me
    If I but call your name?
Will you go where you don't know
    And never be the same?
Will you let my love be shown,
Will you let my name be known,
Will you let my life be grown
    In you and you in me?

2   Will you leave yourself behind
    If I but call your name?
Will you care for cruel and kind
    And never be the same?
Will you risk the hostile stare
Should your life attract or scare?
Will you let me answer prayer
    In you and you in me?

3 Will you let the blinded see
  If I but call your name?
Will you set the prisoners free
  And never be the same?
Will you kiss the leper clean,
And do such as this unseen,
And admit to what I mean
  In you and you in me?

4 Will you love the 'you' you hide
  If I but call your name?
Will you quell the fear inside
  And never be the same?
Will you use the faith you've found
To reshape the world around,
Through my sight and touch and sound
  In you and you in me?

5 Lord, your summons echoes true
  When you but call my name.
Let me turn and follow you
  And never be the same.
In your company I'll go
Where your love and footsteps show.
Thus I'll move and live and grow
  In you and you in me.

JOHN L. BELL b 1949
and GRAHAM MAULE b 1958

PART V

SPECIAL OCCASIONS

IN TIME OF TROUBLE

648

KINGSFOLD DCM

Melody from *English Country Songs* 1893
Harmony by Ralph Vaughan Williams 1872–1958

648 Harmonisation: From *The English Hymnal,* 1906,
Oxford University Press, Great Clarendon Street, Oxford. OX2 6DP. Used by permission.

EARTH'S fragile beauties we possess
　　As pilgrim gifts from God,
And walk the slow and dangerous way
　　His wounded feet have trod.
Though faith by tragedy is rocked,
　　And love with pain is scored,
We sing the pilgrims' song of hope:
　　'Your kingdom come, O Lord!'

2　　Earth's human longings we possess
　　　　By love or grief compelled
To take and bear the heavy cross
　　　Christ's wounded hands have held.
By cloud and fire he leads us on
　　　Through famine, plague or sword,
Singing with faith the pilgrims' song:
　　　'Your kingdom come, O Lord!'

3　　God's own true image we possess
　　　　In innocence first known,
Now tainted by the hate and spite
　　　To Christ's own body shown.
By that same wounded heart of love
　　　God's image is restored,
To sing again the pilgrims' song:
　　　'Your kingdom come, O Lord!'

ROBERT WILLIS b 1947

PART VI

CHURCH AND PEOPLE

649   First Version

PEMBROKE   86 86 88   Patrick Hadley 1899–1973

Unison

Second Version

PEMBROKE   86 86 88   Patrick Hadley 1899–1973
Arranged by Michael Fleming 1928–2006

HOW shall they hear the word of God
    Unless the truth is told;
How shall the sinful be set free,
    The sorrowful consoled?
To all who speak the truth today
    Impart your Spirit, Lord, we pray.

2   How shall they call to God for help
    Unless they have believed;
How shall the poor be given hope,
    The prisoners reprieved?
To those who help the blind to see
    Give light and love and charity.

3   How shall the gospel be proclaimed
    That sinners may repent;
How shall the world find peace at last
    If heralds are not sent?
So send us, Lord, for we rejoice
    To speak of Christ with life and voice.

MICHAEL PERRY 1942–96

650

WOLVERCOTE   76 76 D   William Harold Ferguson 1874–1950

Unison

'THE kingdom is upon you!'
  The voice of Jesus cries,
Fulfilling with its message
  The wisdom of the wise;
It lightens with fresh insight
  The striving human mind,
Creating new dimensions
  Of faith for all to find.

2   'God's kingdom is upon you!'
  The message sounds today,
It summons every pilgrim
  To take the questing way,
With eyes intent on Jesus,
  Our leader and our friend,
Who trod faith's road before us,
  And trod it to the end.

3   The kingdom is upon us!
  Stirred by the Spirit's breath,
We glory in its freedom
  From emptiness and death;
We celebrate its purpose,
  Its mission and its goal,
Alive with the conviction
  That Christ can make us whole.

ROBERT WILLIS b 1947

PART VII

LITURGICAL SECTION

CONTENTS

As in *The New English Hymnal*, the liturgical section is arranged seasonally with music for texts from the *Common Worship* provision, including Times and Seasons. There then follows material for the Eucharist, increasing the scope and provision of that provided in *New English Hymnal*.

First, comes a substantial provision of responsorial material – psalms and canticles. This is primarily for use between the first and second readings of scripture at the Eucharist. The choir, or a cantor, sings the response, which is then repeated by the congregation. The verses follow. After each verse, the congregation sings the response. Most, but not all, of the treatments set the psalm verses to a tone; in these cases, the mark | in the verse indicates the point at which the tone's reciting note is left for the remaining three notes of each phrase. The final stressed syllable of each line should coincide with the last of these notes, and any remaining syllables should be sung lightly on the same note.

A decision has been made to represent plainchant, especially melismatic chant notated in neumes, by means of crotchet noteheads on a 5-line stave with key-signatures. In accordance with current practice when rendering the chant in this manner, the original neumes are denoted by slurs. The beaming in the organ accompaniment melody is arranged by syllabic stress. While this is a departure from the *English Hymnal* tradition, it is hoped that such a means will bring this matchless ancient music of the church to a wider constituency; certainly, the crotchet noteheads with slurs facilitate ease of singing equal to, and perhaps greater than, that obtained by the use of beamed quavers of modern notation.

The editors are grateful to composers and copyright holders for permission to include their work, and particularly to Colin Mawby for his ready response to compose responsorial settings of *Magnificat* and *Benedictus Dominus Deus Israel* especially for *New English Praise*.

Where no composer is listed, musical settings for many of the antiphons and psalm tones are by Simon Lindley and follow in the tradition of the contemporary chant styles of Bevenot, Gelineau and Murray; he also adapted the Great Advent Antiphons to the *Common Worship* texts in contemporary language and, with Michael Fleming, oversaw the compilation of the music for the liturgical section.

Settings by Philip Duffy, Joseph Gelineau and Colin Mawby have been provided for festal use by choir as well as congregation – all this material can easily be sung by unison voices with accompaniment rather than by a four-part choir. Brass Parts to Psalm 150 are available from GIA Chicago. Where such through-composed settings incorporate a Gloria Patri, an indication has been provided for their use as a eucharistic Gradual – for which, by tradition, no Gloria Patri is required.

The adaptation of his music for the Reproaches in *The New English Hymnal* to the new words and the new texts of material for Candlemas and Good Friday was completed by our friend and colleague Michael Fleming shortly before his death.

The editors acknowledge with special gratitude the ready and expert advice on the chanted material in this section given by Andrew Parker.

651

THE GREAT ADVENT ANTIPHONS

1 *O Sapientia :* December 17   Mode ii

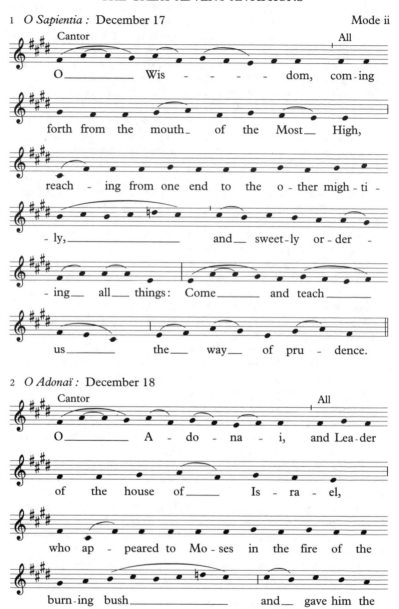

Cantor — All

O_____ Wis - - - - dom, com-ing forth from the mouth_ of the Most_ High, reach - ing from one end to the o - ther migh - ti - ly,_____ and_ sweet-ly or - der - ing_ all_ things : Come_____ and teach_____ us_____ the_ way_ of pru - dence.

2 *O Adonaï :* December 18

Cantor — All

O_____ A - do - na - i, and Lea-der of the house of_____ Is - ra - el, who ap - peared to Mo - ses in the fire of the burn-ing bush_____ and_ gave him the

law_ on_ Si - nai: Come____ and_ re -

- deem____ us____ with an out - stretched arm.

3 *O Radix Jesse :* December 19

Cantor   All

O____ Root_ of__ Jes - se, stand-ing

as a sign a - mong the_ peo - ples; be - fore_ you

kings _ will shut their mouths,_____ to you _ the

na-tions will_ make their_____ prayer: Come__ and de -

- li - ver_ us, and de - lay_ no_ long - er.

4 *O Clavis David :* December 20

Cantor

O_____ Key_ of__ Da - - vid

All

and Scep - tre of the house of__ Is - ra - el;

you o - pen and no one can_ shut;_____

651

you_ shut _ and no_ one_ can o - - pen:

Come_____ and lead the pri - - son - ers

from__ the pri - son - - - house,

those_ who dwell____ in__ dark - ness, ____

and the sha - - dow of ____ death.

5 *O Oriens :* December 21

Cantor

O_____ Morn - - ing___ Star,

All

Splen - dour of Light__ e - - ter - - nal

and Sun __ of righ-teous-ness : _____

Come_ and__ en - - light - - en

those_ who dwell____ in__ dark - ness, ____

and the sha - - dow of ____ death.

6 *O Rex Gentium :* December 22

Cantor

O _____ King of the ___ na - tions, and ___ their ___ De-sire;

All

the Cor - - ner - - stone, _____

mak - - ing ___ both ___ one : _____

Come _____ and save the hu - man ___ race, ____

which you fa - - shioned from ___ clay.

7 *O Emmanuel :* December 23

Cantor

O _____ Em - - ma - - nu - - el,

All

our King and our _____ Law - giv - er,

the Hope ___ of the ___ na - tions _____

and ___ their ___ Sa - - - - viour :

Come _____ and save _____ us _____

O _____ Lord, ___ our _____ God.

651

1 *O Sapientia* (December 17)
O Wisdom, coming forth from the mouth of the Most High,
and reaching from one end to the other mightily,
and sweetly ordering all things:
Come and teach us the way of prudence.

2 *O Adonaï* (December 18)
O Adonaï, and leader of the house of Israel,
who appeared to Moses in the fire of the burning bush
and gave him the law on Sinai:
Come and redeem us with an outstretched arm.

3 *O Radix Jesse* (December 19)
O Root of Jesse, standing as a sign among the peoples;
before you kings will shut their mouths,
to you the nations will make their prayer:
Come and deliver us, and delay no longer.

4 *O Clavis David* (December 20)
O Key of David and Sceptre of the house of Israel;
you open and no one can shut; you shut and no one can open:
Come, and lead the prisoners from the prison-house,
those who dwell in darkness and the shadow of death.

5 *O Oriens* (December 21)
O Morning Star, Splendour of Light eternal and Sun of righteousness:
Come and enlighten those who dwell in darkness
and the shadow of death.

6 *O Rex Gentium* (December 22)
O King of the nations, and their Desire;
the Corner-stone, making both one:
Come and save the human race, which you fashioned from clay.

7 *O Emmanuel* (December 23)
O Emmanuel, our King and our Lawgiver,
the Hope of the nations, and their Saviour:
Come and save us, O Lord our God.

Latin, pre-6th century
Tr Common Worship: Daily Prayer, 2005

652

MAGNIFICAT

Tone ii Solemn

*The antiphons at 651 are sung before and after this canticle:
the intonation is used in every verse, except verses 2 and 5.*

Magnificat

1   Mÿ sóul proclaims *the* great-ness of the Lord : my spí-rit rejoices
in *God* my Sav-iour;

2   [ ] He *has* looked with fa-vour : ón his *low*-ly ser-vant.

3   From this dáy all generations *will* call me bles-sed : the Al-mígh-ty
has done great things for me * and *ho*-ly is his name.

4   He has mér-cy *on* those who fear him : from ge-né-ration
to *ge*-ne-ra-tion.

5   [ ] He has *shown* strength with his arm : and has scát-tered the *proud*
in their con-ceit,

6   Casting dówn *the* might-y from their thrones : ánd líft-ing *up*
the low-ly.

7   He has filled the *hun*-gry with good things : and sent thé
rich *a*-way emp-ty.

8   He has cóme to the aid of *his* ser-vant Is-ra-el : to re-mém-ber his
pro-*mise* of mer-cy,

9   Thë pró-mise *made* to our an-ces-tors : to Á-braham and his
child-*ren* for ev-er.

Glo-ry tó the *Fa*-ther and to the Son : and tó the *Ho*-ly Spi-rit.

As it wás *in* the be-gin-ning : is nów and shall be for *ev*-er. A-men.

Repeat Antiphon full.

Common Worship, 2000

652 Words: © The Archbishops' Council, Church House, Great Smith Street, London SW1P 3NZ.

653

THE BAPTISM OF CHRIST

*One of the following items 653 to 655 may be sung, on this feast and at other
times, whle the congregation is sprinkled with baptismal water.*

ASPERGES ME

Mode vii, 13th century

Cantor: Thou shalt purge me, O

All: Lord, with hys - sop, and I shall be clean: thou shalt wash me, and I shall be whi - ter than snow. *Fine*

Cantor: Have mer - cy up - on me, O God:

All: af - - ter thy great good - - ness.

Cantor: Glo - - ry be to the Father and to the Son; and to the

All: Ho - ly Ghost; As it was in the beginning is now and ev - er shall be: world with - out end. A - men.

Latin, Psalm 51 v. 7

The antiphon may be repeated, or it may be sung once, omitting the 'Gloria Patri'.

Thou shalt purge me, * O Lord, with hyssop, and I shall be clean:
thou shalt wash me, and I shall be whiter than snow.
Ps. Have mercy upon me, O God: after thy great goodness.
V. Glory be to the Father, and to the Son; and to the Holy Ghost;
R. As it was in the beginning, is now, and ever shall be:
  world without end. Amen.
Thou shalt purge me ...

Latin, Psalm 51 v. 7

654

AT THE EASTER LITURGY
and in Eastertide

VIDI AQUAM

Mode viii, 10th century

I be-held____ wa - - ter, which pro - -
-ceed-ed__ out__ of__ the tem - - ple,____
on the__ right____ side__ there - - of,__
Al-le - - lu - - - ya:__ and__ all____
they to__ whom that wa - - ter__ came____
____ were heal - - ed ev - -
- ery____ one: and__ they____ say,__ Al - le -

continued overleaf

- lu - - ya, Al - - le - - - lu - - ya.

Cantor

O give thanks unto the Lord for__ he__ is gra - cious:

All

and__ his__ mercy en - du - reth for__ ev - er. Glo-ry__ be__

Cantor

to the Father and to the Son and__ to__ the Ho - ly Ghost;

All

As__ it__ was in the beginning is now and__ ev - er

shall__ be: world with - - out__ end.__ A - men.

Latin, Ezekiel 47

The antiphon may be repeated, or it may be sung once, omitting the 'Gloria Patri'.

    I beheld water, * which proceeded out of the temple, on the right
       side thereof, Alleluya:
    and all they to whom that water came were healed every one;
    and they say, Alleluya, Alleluya.
    Ps. O give thanks unto the Lord, for he is gracious:
       and his mercy endureth for ever.
    V. Glory be to the Father, and to the Son; and to the Holy Ghost;
    R. As it was in the beginning, is now, and ever shall be:
       world without end. Amen.
    I saw water ...

Latin, Ezekiel 47

655

Stephen Dean b 1948

Water of Life, cleanse and refresh us:
Raise us to life in Christ Jesus.

1   All you who thirst, come to the waters;
     And you will never be thirsty again.

2   As rain from heaven, so is God's word,
     It waters the earth and brings forth life.

3   Dying with Christ, so we shall rise with him,
     Death shall no longer have power over us.

4   Turn to the Lord, cast off your wickedness,
     You will find peace in his infinite love.

STEPHEN DEAN b 1948

655 Words and Music: © 1982 Stephen Dean, OCP Publications, 5536 NE Hassalo, Portland, OR 97213, USA.
All rights reserved. Used with permission.

656

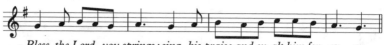

Bless the Lord you springs: sing his praise and ex-alt him for ev - er.

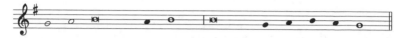

Bless the Lord you springs:
sing his praise and exalt him for ever.

1   Bless the Lord you waters above the *hea*-vens :
      sing his praise and ex-*alt* him for ev-er.
    Bless the Lord sun *and* moon :
      bless the Lord you *stars* öf hea-ven;

2   Bless the Lord all rain *and* dew :
      sing his praise and ex-*alt* him for ev-er.
    Bless the Lord *you* springs :
      bless the Lord you *seas* änd ri-vers;

3   Bless the Lord you servants of *the* Lord :
      sing his praise and ex-*alt* him for ev-er.

based on the Benedicite,
Common Worship, 2000

CANDLEMAS

Mode viii

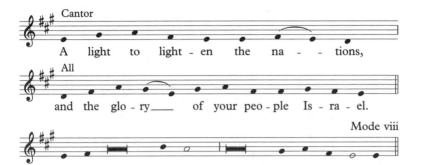

A light to lighten the nations : and the glory of your people Israel.

1   Now Lord you let your servant go in *peace* **:**
     your *word* has been ful-filled.

2   My own eyes have seen the sal-*va*-tion **:** which you have prepared
     in the sight of *ev*-ery peo-ple.

3   A light to reveal you to the *na*-tions **:** and the glory of your *peo*-ple
     Is-ra-el.

     Glory to the Father and to the *Son* **:** and to the *Ho*-ly Spi-rit:
     As it was in the beginning is *now* **:** and shall be for *ev*-er. A-men.

Nunc Dimittis, *Common Worship*, 2000

658

ASH WEDNESDAY

Tone iv.4

Psalm 51

Miserere mei, Deus

1 Have mercy upon me O God * after *thy* great goodness :
according to the multitude of thy mercies do a-*way* mine
of-fen-ces.

2 Wash me throughly *from* my wick-ed-ness :
[ ] *and* cleanse me from my sin.

3 For I acknow-*ledge* my faults :
and my sin is *ev*-er be-fore me.

4 Against thee only have I sinned and done this evil *in* thy sight :
that thou mightest be justified in thy saying * and clear *when*
thou art judg-ed.

5 Behold I was sha-*pen* in wick-ed-ness :
and in sin hath my *mo*-ther con-ceiv-ed-me.

6 But lo thou requirest truth in the *in*-ward parts :
and shalt make me to under-*stand* wis-dom sec-ret-ly.

7 Thou shalt purge me with hyssop and I *shall* be clean :
thou shalt wash me and I shall *be* whi-ter than snow.

8 Thou shalt make me hear of *joy* and glad-ness :
that the bones which thou *hast* bro-ken may re-joice.

9 Turn thy face *from* my sins :
and put *out* all my mis-deeds.

10 Make me a clean *heart* O God :
and renew a right *spi*-rit with-in me.

11 Cast me not away *from* thy pre-sence :
and take not thy ho-*ly* Spi-rit from me.

12 O give me the comfort of thy *help* a-gain :
and stablish me *with* thy free Spi-rit.

13 Then shall I teach thy ways un-*to* the wick-ed :
and sinners shall be *con*-ver-ted un-to thee.

14 Deliver me from blood-guiltiness O God *
thou that art the God *of* my health :
and my tongue shall *sing* of thy right-eous-ness.

15 Thou shalt open my *lips* O Lord :
and *my* mouth shall shew thy praise.

16 For thou desirest no sacrifice else *would* I give it thee :
but thou delightest not *in* bürnt of-fer-ings.

17 The sacrifice of God is a *trou*-bled spirit :
a broken and contrite heart O *God* shalt thou not de-spise.

18 O be favourable and gracious *un*-to Si-on :
build thou the *walls* of Je-ru-sa-lem.

19 Then shalt thou be pleased with the sacrifice of righteousness *
with the burnt-offerings *and* ob-la-tions :
then shall they offer young bullocks *up*-on thine al-tar.

Glory be to the Father and *to* the Son : [ ] *and* to the
Ho-ly Ghost;
As it was in the beginning is now and *ev*-er shall be :
world *with*-out end. A-men.

Psalm 51, *Book of Common Prayer*, 1662

659

ASH WEDNESDAY

The sa - cri - fice of God is a bro - ken spirit.

† *v. 20*

Psalm 51

The sacrifice of God is a broken spirit.

1   Have mercy on me O God in | your great goodness :
     According to the abundance of your compassion blot out |
          my of-fences.

2   Wash me thoroughly | from my wickedness :
     And cleanse me | from my sin.

3   For I acknow-|ledge my faults :
     And my sin is | ever · be-fore me.

4   Against you only have I sinned * and done what is evil |
          in your sight,

5   So that you are justified in your sentence * and righteous |
          in your judgement.

     Refrain

6   I have been wicked even | from my birth :
     A sinner when my | mother · con-ceived me.

7   Behold you desire truth | deep within me :
     And shall make me understand wisdom in the | depths ·
          of my · heart.

8   Purge me with hyssop and I | shall be clean :
     Wash me and I shall be whit-|er than snow.

9   Make me hear of | joy and gladness :
     That the bones you have broken | may re-joice.

     Refrain

10 Turn your | face · from my · sins :
   And blot out all | my mis-deeds.
11 Make me a clean | heart O God :
   And renew a right | spirit · with-in me.

12 Cast me not away | from your presence :
   And take not your holy | spi-rit from me.
13 Give me again the joy of | your sal-vation :
   And sustain me with your | gracious spirit;

Refrain

14 Then shall I teach your | ways . to the . wicked :
   And sinners shall re-|turn to you.
15 Deliver me from my guilt O God * the God of | my sal-vation :
   And my tongue shall | sing · of your · righteousness.

16 O Lord | open · my lips :
   And my mouth shall pro-|claim your praise.
17 For you desire no sacrifice * else | I would give it :
   You take no delight in | burnt offerings.

Refrain

18 The sacrifice of God is a | bro-ken spirit :
   A broken and contrite heart O God you will | not de-spise.
19 O be favourable and | gracious · to Zion :
   Build up the | walls · of Jerusalem.

†20 Then you will accept sacrifices offered in righteousness *
      the burnt offerings | and ob-lations :
   Then shall they offer up bulls | on your altar.

Refrain

Glory to the Father and | to the Son : and to the | Ho-ly Spirit:
As it was in the be-|ginning · is · now : and shall be for ev-|er.
   A-men.

Psalm 51, *Common Worship*, 2000

660

THE REPROACHES

This is the wood of the Cross, on which hung the Saviour of the world. Come, let us wor-ship.

O my_ peo-ple, O my_ church, What have I done to you, or in what have I of-fend-ed you? Tes-ti-fy a-gainst me.

I led you forth from the land of Egypt, and delivered you by the wa-ters of bap-tism, but you have prepared a cross for your Sa-viour._

Ho-ly_ God, ho-ly and strong, ho-ly and im--mort-al, have mer-cy up-on us.

The music continues directly, overleaf

This is the wood of the Cross, on which hung the
    Saviour of the world.
Come, let us worship.

O my people, O my Church,
What have I done to you, or in what have I offended you?
Testify against me.

I led you forth from the land of Egypt,
And delivered you by the waters of baptism,
But you have prepared a cross for your Saviour.

Holy God, holy and strong,
Holy and immortal, have mercy upon us.

I led you through the desert forty years,
And fed you with manna.
I brought you through tribulation and penitence,
And gave you my body, the bread of heaven,
But you prepared a cross for your Saviour.

All repeat: 'Holy God …'

What more could I have done for you
That I have not done?
I planted you, my chosen and fairest vineyard,
I made you the branches of my vine;
But when I was thirsty, you gave me vinegar to drink,
And pierced with a spear the side of your Saviour.

All repeat: 'Holy God …'

Cantor: We glory in your Cross, O Lord:
All: And praise you for your mighty Resurrection,
Cantor: For by virtue of your Cross:
All: Joy has come into our world.

660

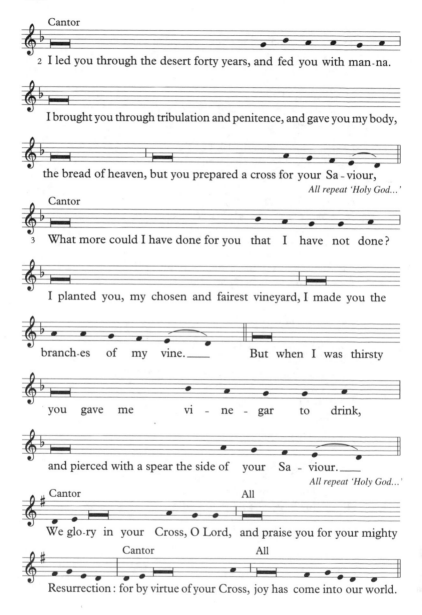

Cantor

2 I led you through the desert forty years, and fed you with man-na.

I brought you through tribulation and penitence, and gave you my body,

the bread of heaven, but you prepared a cross for your Sa - viour,

All repeat 'Holy God...'

Cantor

3 What more could I have done for you that I have not done?

I planted you, my chosen and fairest vineyard, I made you the

branch-es of my vine.___ But when I was thirsty

you gave me vi - ne - gar to drink,

and pierced with a spear the side of your Sa - viour.___

All repeat 'Holy God...'

Cantor   All

We glo-ry in your Cross, O Lord, and praise you for your mighty

Cantor   All

Resurrection: for by virtue of your Cross, joy has come into our world.

Tone vii.2

1 God be gracious to *us* and bless us :
   and make his face to *shine* up-on us,

2 That your way may be *known* up-on earth :
   your saving power a-*mong* all na-tions.

3 Let the peoples *praise* you O God :
   let all the *peo*-ples praise you.

4 O let the nations re-*joice* and be glad :
   for you will judge the peoples righteously *
   and govern the *na*-tions up-on earth.

5 Let the peoples *praise* you O God :
   let all the *peo*-ples praise you.

6 Then shall the earth bring *forth* her in-crease :
   and God our own *God* will bless us.

7 [ ] *God* will bless us :
   and all the ends of the *earth* shall fear him.

All repeat:'We glory in your Cross, O Lord ...'

Common Worship: Times and Seasons, 2006
and *Common Worship,* 2000

661

THE EASTER LITURGY

Suitable texts for singing after the readings will be found at 537, 689, 690 and 530, or, in traditional language, at 518. During the sprinkling of the congregation with baptismal water 654, 655 or 656 may be sung.

SCAMPSTON 10 10 10 10   Richard Shephard b 1948

Exsultet iam angelica turba coelorum

SING, choirs of heaven! Let saints and angels sing!
Around God's throne exult in harmony!
Now Jesus Christ is risen from the grave!
Salute your King in glorious symphony!

2   Sing, choirs of earth! Behold, your light has come!
The glory of the Lord shines radiantly!
Lift up your hearts, for Christ has conquered death!
The night is past: the day of life is here!

3   Sing, Church of God! Exult with joy outpoured!
The gospel trumpets tell of victory won!
Your Saviour lives; he's with you evermore!
Let all God's people sound the long Amen!

Tr Common Worship: Times and Seasons, 2006

662

EASTER ALLELUYAS

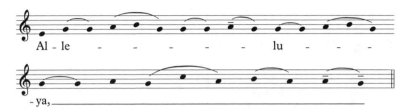

Al - le - - - - - lu - - -
- ya,

*This Alleluya after the Epistle is sung first by the Celebrant, then repeated by
the Congregation. This is done three times, each repetition in a higher key.*

Alternatively, the Alleluya and verse below may be used.

Al - le - lu - ya, Al - le - lu - ya,___ Al - le - lu - ya.

I am the first and the last says the Lord and the li-*ving* one :
I was dead and behold I am a-*live* for e-ver-more.

Common Worship: Times and Seasons, 2006

Al - le - lu - ya, Al - le - lu - ya,___ Al - le - lu - ya.

663

EASTER DISMISSAL

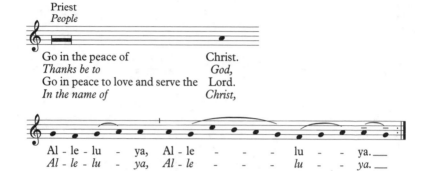

Priest
People

Go in the peace of   Christ.
Thanks be to   *God,*
Go in peace to love and serve the   Lord.
In the name of   *Christ,*

Al - le - lu - ya,   Al - le - lu - ya.__
Al - le - lu - ya,   Al - le - lu - ya.__

Common Worship, 2000

664

CORPUS CHRISTI

LAUDA SION 88 7 D AND 888 7 D   Gerard Francis Cobb 1838–1904

Unison

Lauda Sion salvatorem

Part I

LAUD, O Sion, thy salvation,
Laud with hymns of exultation
    Christ, thy King and Shepherd true:
Spend thyself, his honour raising,
Who surpasseth all thy praising;
    Never canst thou reach his due.

2   Sing today, the mystery showing
Of the living, life-bestowing
    Bread from heaven before thee set;
E'en the same of old provided,
Where the Twelve, divinely guided,
    At the holy Table met.

3   Full and clear ring out thy chanting,
Joy nor sweetest grace be wanting
    To thy heart and soul today;
When we gather up the measure
Of that Supper and its treasure,
    Keeping feast in glad array.

4   Lo, the new King's Table gracing,
This new Passover of blessing
    Hath fulfilled the elder rite:
Now the new the old effaceth,
Truth revealed the shadow chaseth,
    Day is breaking on the night.

5   What he did at Supper seated,
Christ ordained to be repeated,
    His memorial ne'er to cease:
And, his word for guidance taking,
Bread and wine we hallow, making
    Thus our Sacrifice of peace.

continued overleaf

664

6 This the truth to Christians given —
Bread becomes his Flesh from heaven,
 Wine becomes his holy Blood.
Doth it pass thy comprehending?
Yet by faith, thy sight transcending,
 Wondrous things are understood.

7 Yea, beneath these signs are hidden
Glorious things to sight forbidden:
 Look not on the outward sign.
Wine is poured and Bread is broken,
But in either sacred token
 Christ is here by power divine.

8 Whoso of this Food partaketh,
Rendeth not the Lord nor breaketh:
 Christ is whole to all that taste.
Thousands are, as one, receivers,
One, as thousands of believers,
 Takes the Food that cannot waste.

9 Good and evil men are sharing
One repast, a doom preparing
 Varied as the heart of man;
Doom of life or death awarded,
As their days shall be recorded
 Which from one beginning ran.

Part 2

10   WHEN the Sacrament is broken,
     Doubt not in each severed token,
     Hallowed by the word once spoken,
        Resteth all the true content:
     Nought the precious Gift divideth,
     Breaking but the sign betideth,
     He himself the same abideth,
        Nothing of his fullness spent.

11   Lo! the Angels' Food is given
     To the pilgrim who hath striven;
     See the children's Bread from heaven,
        Which to dogs may not be cast;
     Truth the ancient types fulfilling,
     Isaac bound, a victim willing,
     Paschal lamb, its life-blood spilling.
        Manna sent in ages past.

continued overleaf

664

Slower

a tempo e cresc.

cresc.

When used as
Sequence at Mass

A - men.

When used as Sequence at Mass

Al - - le - lu - ya,

Part 3

12   O TRUE Bread, good Shepherd, tend us,
Jesu, of thy love befriend us,
Thou refresh us, thou defend us,
Thine eternal goodness send us
   In the land of life to see;
Thou who all things canst and knowest,
Who on earth such Food bestowest,
Grant us with thy Saints, though lowest,
Where the heavenly Feast thou showest,
   Fellow-heirs and guests to be.
     Amen. Alleluya.

St Thomas Aquinas c 1225–74
Cento

665

CORPUS CHRISTI

Alternative tune for verses 1 to 9 *of* 664

ALLES IST AN GOTTES SEGEN   *Colmarische Gesangbuch*, 1691
88 7 D   Melody by Johann Löhner 1645–1705
Harmony by Johann Sebastian Bach 1685–1750

Lauda Sion salvatorem

Part I

LAUD, O Sion, thy salvation,
Laud with hymns of exultation
   Christ, thy King and Shepherd true:
Spend thyself, his honour raising,
Who surpasseth all thy praising;
   Never canst thou reach his due.

2   Sing today the mystery showing
Of the living, life bestowing
   Bread from heaven before thee set;
E'en the same of old provided,
Where the Twelve, divinely guided,
   At the holy Table met.

3   Full and clear ring out thy chanting,
Joy nor sweetest grace be wanting
   To thy heart and soul today;
When we gather up the measure
Of that Supper and its treasure,
   Keeping feast in glad array.

4   Lo, the new King's Table gracing,
This new Passover of blessing
    Hath fulfilled the elder rite:
Now the new the old effaceth,
Truth revealed the shadow chaseth,
    Day is breaking on the night.

5   What he did at Supper seated,
Christ ordained to be repeated,
    His memorial ne'er to cease:
And, his word for guidance taking,
Bread and wine we hallow, making
    Thus our Sacrifice of peace.

6   This the truth to Christians given —
Bread becomes his Flesh from heaven,
    Wine becomes his holy Blood.
Doth it pass thy comprehending?
Yet by faith, thy sight transcending,
    Wondrous things are understood.

7   Yea, beneath these signs are hidden
Glorious things to sight forbidden:
    Look not on the outward sign.
Wine is poured and Bread is broken,
But in either sacred token
    Christ is here by power divine.

8   Whoso of this Food partaketh,
Rendeth not the Lord nor breaketh:
    Christ is whole to all that taste.
Thousands are, as one, receivers,
One, as thousands of believers,
    Takes the Food that cannot waste.

9   Good and evil men are sharing
One repast, a doom preparing
    Varied as the heart of man;
Doom of life or death awarded,
As their days shall be recorded
    Which from one beginning ran.

ST THOMAS AQUINAS c 1225–74
Cento

This tune is also known as AUCTOR OMNIUM BONORUM *and* EVANGELISTS.

666

GOSPEL ACCLAMATIONS

All seasons outside Lent

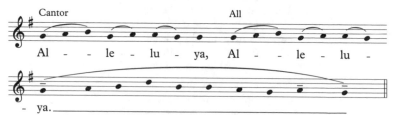

The choir or cantor then sings one of the verses at 667,
following which the Alleluya below is sung by all.

An alternative Alleluya is to be found as the second item at 662.

During Lent

The choir or cantor then sings one of the Lenten verses at 667,
following which the acclamation below is sung by all.

667

Tone vi

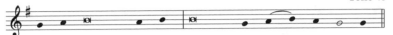

Advent

1   Show us your mercy *O* Lord : and grant us *your* sal-va-tion.

2   Prepare the way of the Lord make his *paths* straight : and all
     flesh shall see the sal-*va*-tion of our Lord.

3   The spirit of the Lord God is upon me because the Lord has
     anoint-*ed* me : he has sent me to bring good *news* to the
     op-pressed.

4   A virgin shall conceive and bear *a* son : and his name shall be
     called Emmanuel * *God* is with us.

Christmas and Epiphany

5   The Word became flesh and dwelt a-*mong* us : and we have *seen*
     his glo-ry.

6   May the peace of Christ reign in *your* hearts : let the message of
     Christ *find* a home in you.

7   We have seen his star at its *ris*-ing : and have come to *pay*
     him ho-mage.

Baptism of Christ and Sunday next before Lent

8   This is my Son, the Be-*lov*-ed : with whom *I* am well pleased.

Candlemas

9   This child is the light to enlighten the *na*-tions : and the glory
     of your *peo*-ple Is-ra-el.

Sundays after Epiphany, see 5, 6 and 31 to 34

continued overleaf

667

Tone vi

Lent

10   The Lord is a great God * O that today you would listen
to *his* voice : hard-*en* not your hearts.

11   We do not live by bread *a*-lone : but by every word that
comes *from* the mouth of God.

12   Blessed are those who have endured temp-*ta*-tion : they have
stood the test and will re-*ceive* the crown of life.

13   God is *spi*-rit : and those who worship him must worship
in *spi*-rit and truth.

14   I am the light of the world says *the* Lord : anyone who follows
me with *have* the light of life.

15   Your word is a lamp to *my* feet : and a *light* to my path.

Palm Sunday

16   Christ humbled himself and became obedient unto death *
even death on *a* cross : therefore God has highly exalted him
and given him the name that is *a*-bove ev-*ery* name.

Maundy Thursday

17   I give to you a new commandment says *the* Lord : love one
another as *I* have loved you.

Easter

18   Jesus said 'All who see the Son and believe in him may have
eter-*nal* life : and I will raise them up *on* the last day.'

19   Jesus said 'You have believed because you have *seen* me :
blessed are those who have not *seen* and yet be-lieve.

20 I am the first and the last says the Lord and the li-*ving* one :
   I was dead and behold I am a-*live* for e-ver-more.

21 Open to us the scriptures *Lord* Christ : make our hearts *burn*
   with-in us.

22 My sheep hear my voice says *the* Lord : I know them *and* they
   fol-low me.

Ascension

23 Go and make disciples of all *na*-tions : for I am with you always *to*
   the end of time.

Pentecost or Whit Sunday

24 Come Holy Spirit, fill the hearts of your faithful *peo*-ple :
   and kindle in them the *fire* of your love.

Trinity Sunday

25 Glory to the Father and to the Son and to the Holy *Spi*-rit :
   one God who was who is and who is to come * *the* Al-migh-ty.

Corpus Christi

26 I am the living bread that came down from heaven says *the* Lord :
   whoever eats of this bread will *live* for ev-er.

All Saints' Day; or any Saint

27 Blessed are the poor in *spi*-rit : for theirs is the king-*dom* of heaven.

Christ the King

28 You Christ are the King of *glo*-ry : the eternal Son *of* the Fa-ther.

Dedication Festival

29 Lord we have loved the habitation of *your* house : and the
   place *where* your glo-ry dwells.

continued overleaf

667

Tone vi

The Blessed Virgin Mary, see 4 or 5 above

Apostles

30   The glorious company of the apostles *praise* you : throughout
     the world the holy *church* ac-claims you.

Sundays after Trinity

(see also 1, 13, 14, 15 and 21)

31   Open our hearts, *O* Lord : to accept the *words* of your Son.

32   I am the way the truth and the life says *the* Lord : no one comes to
     the Fa-*ther* ex-cept through me.

33   Your words are spirit Lord and they *are* life : you have the
     message *of* e-ter-nal life.

34   Speak Lord for your servant is *list*-en-ing : you have the
     words *of* e-ter-nal life.

Acclamations 5, 11, 20, 22–25, 32, 34:
Common Worship, 2000
Acclamations 7–10, 12, 15–18, 26–29:
Common Worship: Times and Seasons, 2006

668

Antiphon and Tone by Joseph Gelineau, SJ b 1920

How great is your name, O Lord our God, — through all the earth!

Psalm 8

How great is your name, O Lord our God, through all the earth!

1   Your majesty above the | heavens is praised
    Out of the mouths of babes | at the breast.
    You have founded a stronghold a-|gainst your foes,
    That you might still the enemy | and · the a-venger.

2   When I consider your heavens * the work | of your fingers,
    The moon and the stars that | you · have or-dained,
    What is man that you should be mind-|ful of him;
    The son of man that you should | seek him out?

3   You have made him little | lower · than the · angels
    And crown him with | glory · and honour.
    You have given him dominion over the | works · of your · hands
    And put all things | under · his feet,

4   All | sheep and oxen,
    Even the wild | beasts · of the · field,
    The birds of the air * the | fish · of the · sea
    And whatsoever moves in the | paths · of the · sea.

The Grail, 1963
JOSEPH GELINEAU, SJ   b 1920

668   Music: © 1984 Kevin Mayhew Ltd, Buxhall, Stowmarket, Suffolk.   IP14 3BW   Used by permission.
668   Words: © Set to music and reproduced by permission of The Grail, England.
Administered by A. P. Watt Ltd., 20 John Street, London.   WC1N 2DR

669

The just will live in the pre-sence of the Lord.

Psalm 15

The just will live in the presence of the Lord.

1   Lord who may dwell | in your tabernacle?
    Who may rest upon your | ho-ly hill?
    Whoever leads an | uncor-rupt life,
    And does the | thing · that is · right;

2   Who speaks the | truth · from the · heart,
    And bears no deceit | on the tongue;
    Who does no evil | to a friend,
    And pours no scorn | on a neighbour;

3   In whose sight the wicked are | not es-teemed,
    But who honours those who | fear the Lord.
    Whoever has | sworn · to a · neighbour
    And never goes | back · on that · word;

4   Who does not lend money in | hope of gain,
    Nor takes a bribe a-|gainst the innocent;
    Whoever | does these things
    Shall | ne-ver fall.

Common Worship, 2000

The Antiphon at the foot of the page is sung before verse 1.

Joseph Gelineau, SJ b 1920

Steadily

1 The Lord is my shepherd;
2 He guides me a-long the right path;
3 You have pre-pared a banquet for me
4 Surely goodness and kindness shall follow me

there is nothing I shall want.
he is true to his name.
in the sight of my foes. If I should
all the days of my life. My

In the

Fresh and green are the pastures where he
walk in the valley of darkness no
head you have a-nointed with oil;
Lord's own house shall I dwell

(1) gives me re-pose. Near restful waters he
(2) evil would I fear. You are there with your crook and your

leads me, to re-vive my drooping spi - - rit.
staff; with these you give me com - fort.
(3) my cup is o-ver-flow - ing.
(4) for ev - - er and ev - - er.

Antiphon *(Crotchet equals minim pulse of Psalm.)*

The Lord is my Shep-herd, no-thing shall I want; He

leads me by safe paths, no-thing shall I fear.

Psalm 23

The Lord is my shepherd, nothing shall I want:
He leads me by safe paths, nothing shall I fear.

1 The | Lord is my | shepherd * there is | nothing I shall want.
| Fresh and | green are the | pastures * where he | gives me |
repose.
Near | restful | waters he | leads me * to re-|vive my drooping |
spirit.

2 He | guides me a-|long the right | path * he is | true to his | name.
If I should | walk in the | valley of | darkness * no | evil · would I |
fear.
You are | there with your | crook and your | staff * with | these you
give me | comfort.

3 You have pre-|pared a | banquet for | me * in the | sight · of my
foes.
My | head you have a-|nointed with | oil * my | cup is over-|flowing.

4 Surely | goodness and | kindness shall | follow me * all the | days ·
of my | life.
In the | Lord's own | house shall I | dwell * for | ëv-er and | ever.

The Grail, 1963
JOSEPH GELINEAU, SJ   b 1920

670   Words: © Set to music and reproduced by permission of The Grail, England.
Administered by A. P. Watt Ltd., 20 John Street, London. WC1N 2DR

671

Ian Forrester

The Lord will bless his peo-ple with peace.

Anthony Gregory Murray 1905–92

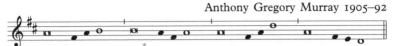

Psalm 29

The Lord will bless his people with peace.

1   Ascribe to the Lord you | powers of heaven,
Ascribe to the Lord | glory · and strength.
Ascribe to the Lord the honour | due un-to his name;
Worship the Lord in the | beauty · of holiness.

2   The voice of the Lord is up-|on the waters,
The God of | glo-ry thunders,
The Lord is upon the mighty waters * the voice of the
     Lord is mighty in | ope-ration;
The voice of the Lord is a | glori-ous voice.

3   The Lord sits enthroned a-|bove the water-flood;
The Lord sits enthroned as king for | evermore.
The Lord shall give | strength · to his · people;
The Lord shall give his people the | blessing · of peace.

Psalm 29, vv. 1–4, 9, 10, *Common Worship*, 2000

672

I will ex - alt you, O Lord, be-cause you have raised me up,

† v. 6

Psalm 30

I will exalt you, O Lord, because you have raised me up.

1   I will exalt you O Lord because you have | raised me up,
And have not let my foes | tri-umph over me.
O Lord my God I cried | out to you,
And | you have healed me.

2   You brought me up O Lord | from the dead;
You restored me to life from among those that go | down ·
     to the · Pit.
Sing to the Lord you | servants · of his;
Give thanks to his | holy name.

3   For his wrath endures but the | twinkling · of an · eye,
His favour | for a lifetime.
Heaviness may en-|dure · for a · night,
But joy comes | in the morning.

4   In my prosperity I said 'I shall | never be moved.
You Lord of your goodness have made my | hill so strong.'
Then you | hid your face from me
And I was | utter-ly dis-mayed.

5   To you O | Lord I cried;
To the Lord I made my | suppli-cation.
'What profit is there in my blood if I go | down · to the · Pit?
Will the dust praise you or de-|clare your faithfulness?

†6   'Hear O Lord and have | mercy · up-on me;
O Lord | be my helper.

7   You have turned my mourning | in-to dancing;
You have put off my sackcloth and girded | me with gladness;
Therefore my heart sings to you | with-out ceasing;
O Lord my God I will give you | thanks for ever.

Common Worship, 2000

My trust is in you, O Lord: you are my God.

Psalm 31

My trust is in you, O Lord: you are my God.

1 Have mercy on me, Lord * for | I · am in · trouble;
My eye is consumed with sorrow * my soul and my |
   bo-dy also.
For my life is wasted with grief and my | years with sighing;
My strength fails me because of my affliction * and my |
   bones · are con-sumed.

2 I have become a reproach to all my enemies and even to my
      neighbours * an object of dread to | my ac-quaintances;
When they see me in the street they | flëe from me.
I am forgotten like one that is dead | out of mind;
I have become like a | brok-en vessel.

3 For I have heard the whispering of the crowd * fear is on |
      every side;
They scheme together against me and plot to | take my life.
But my trust is in | you O Lord
I have said | 'You · are my · God.'

4 'My times are | in your hand;
Deliver me from the hand of my enemies * and from | those
   who persecute me.
Make your face to shine up-|on your servant,
And save me for your | mercy's sake.'

Psalm 31, vv. 9–16, *Common Worship*, 2000

674

On your right stands the␣ Queen in gar - ments of gold.

Psalm 45

On your right stands the Queen in garments of gold.

1   Hear O daughter * consider and in-|cline your ear;
Forget your own people and your | Father's house.
So shall the king have | pleasure • in your • beauty;
He is your lord so | do him honour.

2   The people of Tyre shall | bring you gifts;
The richest of the people shall | seek your favour.
The king's daughter is all | glorious with-in;
Her clothing is embroidered | cloth of gold.

3   She shall be brought to the king in | raiment • of needlework;
After her virgins that are | her com-panions.
With joy and gladness shall | they be brought
And enter into the | palace • of the • king.

4   'Instead of your fathers you | shall have sons,
Whom you shall make princes over | all the land.
I will make your name to be remembered through all |
     gener-ations;
Therefore shall the peoples praise you for | ever • and ever.'

Psalm 45, vv. 10–17, *Common Worship,* 2000

675

The morn-ing and the eve-ning sing your praise.

Anthony Gregory Murray 1905–92
†v. 3

Psalm 65

The morning and the evening sing your praise.

1 Praise is due to you O | God in Zion;
   To you that answer prayer shall | vows be paid.
   To you shall all flesh come to con-|fess their sins;
   When our misdeeds prevail against us you will |
       purge · them a-way.

2 In your strength you set | fast the mountains
   And are girded a-|bout with might.
   You still the | raging · of the · seas,
   The roaring of their waves and the | clamour · of the ·
       peoples.

†3 Those who dwell at the ends of the earth | tremble ·
       at your · marvels;
   The gates of the morning and evening | sing your praise.

Psalm 65, vv. 1, 2, 5–7, *Common Worship,* 2000

676

Some seed fell in rich soil and blos-somed with a - bun - dance.

Anthony Gregory Murray 1905–92

Psalm 65

Some seed fell in rich soil and blossomed with abundance.

1   You visit the | earth and water it;
       You make it | ve-ry plenteous.
       The river of God is | full of water;
       You prepare grain for your people * for so you pro-|vide ·
         for the · earth.

2   You drench the furrows and smooth | out the ridges;
       You soften the ground with showers and | bless its increase.
       You crown the year | with your goodness,
       And your paths over-|flow with plenty.

3   May the pasture of the wilderness | flow with goodness,
       And the hills be | girded with joy.
       May the meadows be clothed with | flocks of sheep
       And the valleys stand so thick with corn that they shall |
         laugh and sing.

Psalm 65, vv. 8–13, *Common Worship,* 2000

677

All na-tions shall fall be-fore you, O Lord, our God.

Laurence Bevenot 1901–90

Psalm 72

All nations shall fall before you, O Lord, our God.

1   Give the king your | judgements · O God,
And your righteousness to the son | of a king.
Then shall he judge your | peo-ple righteously
And your | poor with justice.

2   The kings of Tarshish and of the isles | shall pay tribute;
The kings of Sheba and Seba | shall bring gifts.
All kings shall fall | down be-fore him;
All nations shall | do him service.

3   For he shall deliver the poor | that cry out,
The needy and those who | have no helper.
He shall have pity on the | weak and poor;
He shall preserve the lives | of the needy.

4   He shall redeem their lives from op-|pression and violence,
And dear shall their blood be | in his sight.
Long may he live * unto him may be given | gold from Sheba;
May prayer be made for him continually * and may they bless
him | all the · day long.

Psalm 72, vv. 1, 2, 10–15, *Common Worship*, 2000

678

Antiphon and Tone by
Anthony Gregory Murray 1905–92

God of hosts, bring us back: let your face shine on   us and we shall be saved.

Psalm 80

*God of hosts, bring us back : let your face shine on us and we
shall be saved.*

1   Hear O | Shepherd of Israel,
You that led Joseph | like a flock;
Shine forth you that are enthroned up-|on the cherubim,
Before Ephraim Benjamin | and Ma-nasseh.

2   Stir up your | mighty strength
And come to | our sal-vation.
O Lord | God of hosts,
How long will you be angry at your | people's prayer?

3   You feed them with the | bread of tears;
You give them abundance of | tears to drink.
You have made us the derision | of our neighbours,
And our enemies laugh | us to scorn.

Psalm 80, vv. 1–3, 5–7, *Common Worship,* 2000

679

His an - gels keep you in all your ways.

†v. 5

Psalm 91

His angels keep you in all your ways.

1   Whoever dwells in the shelter of │ the Most High
    And abides under the shadow of │ the Almighty,
    Shall say to the Lord, 'My refuge │ and my stronghold,
    My God in whom I │ put my trust.'

2   There shall no evil │ happen to you,
    Neither shall any plague come │ near your tent.
    For he shall give his angels │ charge over you,
    To keep you in │ all your ways.

3   They shall bear you │ in their hands,
    Lest you dash your foot a-│gainst a stone.
    You shall tread upon the │ lion and adder;
    The young lion and the serpent you shall trample │ underfoot.

4   Because they have set their love upon me *   therefore will │
        I de-liver them;
    I will lift them up because they │ know my name.
    They will call upon me and │ I will answer them;
    I am with them in trouble *   I will deliver them and bring │
        them to honour.

†5 With long life │ will I satisfy them
    And show them │ my sal-vation.

Psalm 91, vv. 1, 2, 10–16, *Common Worship,* 2000

680

The Lord is king, with ma-jes-ty en-robed.

Psalm 93

The Lord is king, with majesty enrobed.

1 The Lord is king and has put on │ glorious ap-parel;
 The Lord has put on his glory and girded him-│self with strength.
 He has made the whole │ world so sure
 That it │ cannot · be moved.

2 Your throne has been established │ from of old;
 You are from │ ev-er-lasting.
 The floods have lifted up O Lord * the floods have lifted │
  up their voice;
 The floods lift up their │ pounding waves.

3 Mightier than the thunder of many waters * mightier than the │
  breakers · of the sea,
 The Lord on │ high is mightier.
 Your testimonies are │ very sure;
 Holiness adorns your house O │ Lord for ever.

Common Worship, 2000

680 Music: © The English Hymnal Company Ltd
680 Words: © The Archbishops' Council, Church House, Great Smith Street, London SW1P 3NZ.

681

Ex - alt the Lord our God, for he____ is__ ho - ly.

Psalm 99

Exalt the Lord our God, for he is holy.

1   The Lord is king * let the | peoples tremble;
    He is enthroned above the cherubim * let the | eärth shake.
    The Lord is | great in Zion
    And high a-|bove all peoples.

2   Let them praise your name which is | great and awesome;
    The Lord our | God is holy.
    Mighty king who loves justice * you have e-|stab-lished equity;
    You have executed justice and | righteous-ness in · Jacob.

3   Moses and Aaron among his priests * and Samuel among those
        who call up-|on his name;
    They called upon the Lord | and he answered them.
    He spoke to them out of the | pillar of cloud;
    They kept his testimonies and the | law · that he · gave them.

4   You answered them O | Lord our God;
    You were a God who forgave them and pardoned them for |
        their of-fences.
    Exalt the Lord our God * and worship him upon his | holy hill,
    For the Lord our | God is holy.

Common Worship, 2000

681   Music: © The English Hymnal Company Ltd
681   Words: © The Archbishops' Council, Church House, Great Smith Street, London SW1P 3NZ.

682

Colin Mawby b 1936

Antiphon

God made us; we be-long____ to__ him.

Psalm *Unison*

Cry out with joy to the Lord, all the earth. Serve the__

Lord with glad-ness. Come be-fore him, sing-ing for joy.

Antiphon

God made us; we be-long____ to__ him.

Psalm *Unison*

Know that he, the Lord, is__ God. He made us,__ we be-

-long to him, we are his peo-ple, the sheep of his flock.

Antiphon

God made us; we be-long____ to__ him.

Psalm *Unison (Tenors & Basses)*

Go with-in his gates, giv-ing__ thanks. En-ter his

682

courts with songs of praise. Give thanks to him and bless his name.

Antiphon   Psalm

God made us; we be-long___ to__ him.

Unison

In -

(Soprano)

In-deed, how good is the Lord, e - ter-nal his mer-ci-ful

deed, how good is the Lord, e - ter-nal his mer-ci-ful

love. He__ is faith - ful from age to__ age.

love. He is faith - ful from age to age.

to ✠ when used at the Gradual

Antiphon

God made us; we be - long___ to __

Doxology

him. Give glo-ry to the Fa - ther Al-migh - ty, to his

Son Je - sus Christ, the Lord, to the Spi - rit who

dwells___ in our hearts. *God made*
us; we be - long_____ to___ him.

Psalm 100

God made us, we belong to him.

1   Cry out with joy to the Lord, all the earth.
Serve the Lord with gladness.
Come before him, singing for joy.

2   Know that he, the Lord, is God.
He made us, we belong to him,
We are his people, the sheep of his flock.

3   Go within his gates, giving thanks.
Enter his courts with songs of praise.
Give thanks to him and bless his name.

4   Indeed, how good is the Lord,
eternal his merciful love.
He is faithful from age to age.

The Grail, 1963

682 Words: © Set to music and reproduced by permission of The Grail, England.
Administered by A. P. Watt Ltd., 20 John Street, London. WC1N 2DR

683

The praise of the Lord en-dures for_ ev - er, Al - le - lu - ya!

Psalm 111

The praise of the Lord endures for ever, Alleluya!

1   I will give thanks to the Lord with my | whöle heart,
In the company of the faithful and in the | con-gregation.
The works of the | Lord are great,
Sought out by all who de-|light in them.

2   His work is full of | majesty · and honour
And his righteousness en-|dures for ever.
He appointed a memorial for his | marvel-lous deeds;
The Lord is gracious and | full of · com-passion.

3   He gave food to | those who feared him;
He is ever mindful | of his covenant.
He showed his people the | power · of his · works
In giving them the heritage | of the nations.

4   The works of his hands are | truth and justice;
All his com-|mandments are sure.
They stand fast for | ever and ever;
They are done in | truth and equity.

5   He sent redemption to his people * he commanded his |
        covenant · for ever;
Holy and awesome | is his name.
The fear of the Lord is the be-|ginning of wisdom;
A good understanding have those who live by it *
        his praise en-|dures for ever.

Common Worship, 2000

683 Music: © The English Hymnal Company Ltd
683 Words: © The Archbishops' Council, Church House, Great Smith Street, London SW1P 3NZ.

My help comes from the Lord, who made heaven and earth.

Psalm 121

*My help comes from the Lord, who made
heaven and earth.*

1 I lift up my eyes | to the hills;
From where is my | help to come?
My help comes | from the Lord,
The maker of | heav'n and earth.

2 He will not suffer your | foot to stumble;
He who watches over you | will not sleep.
Behold he who keeps watch | over Israel
Shall neither slum-|ber nor sleep.

3 The Lord himself | watches over you;
The Lord is your shade at | your right hand,
So that the sun shall not strike | you by day,
Neither the | moon by night.

4 The Lord shall keep you | from all evil;
It is he who shall | keep your soul.
The Lord shall keep watch over your going
  out and your | coming in,
From this time forth for | evermore.

Common Worship, 2000

685

Fintan O'Carroll d 1977

What mar-vels the Lord worked for us, in-deed we were glad.

Anthony Gregory Murray 1905–92

Psalm 126

What marvels the Lord worked for us, indeed we were glad.

1 When the Lord restored the | fortunes · of Zion,
Then were we like | those who dream.
Then was our mouth | filled with laughter,
And our tongue with | songs of joy.

2 Then said they a-|mong the nations,
The Lord has | done great things for them.
The Lord has indeed | done great things for us,
And therefore | we rejoiced.

3 Restore again our | fortunes · O Lord,
As the river beds | of the desert.
Those who | sow in tears
Shall reap with | songs of joy.

4 Those who | go out weeping
Bear-|ing the seed,
Will come back with | shouts of joy,
Bringing their | shëaves · with them.

Common Worship, 2000

686

Joseph Gelineau, SJ b 1920

Great is his love, love with-out end.

Great is his love, love with-out end.

Great is his love, love with-out end.

Psalm 136

1 O give | thanks to the | Lord for · he is | good
Great is his | love, love without | end.
Give | thanks to the | God of | gods
Great is his | love, love without | end.
Give | thanks to the | Lörd of | lords,
Great is his | love, love without | end.

2 Who a-|lone has wrought | mar-vel-lous | works,
Whose | wisdom it | was made the | skies,
Who fixed the earth | firmly on the seas,

3 It was he who | made the great | lights,
The | sun to | rule · in the | day,
The | moon and the | stars in the | night,

4 Thë | first-born of the E-|gypt-ians he | smote,
He brought | Israel | out from the | midst,
Arm out-|stretched with | power in his | hand,

5 He di-|vided the | Red Sea in | two,
He made | Israel | pass through the |midst,
He flung | Pharaoh and his | force in the | sea,

continued overleaf

686

(omit v. 6)

Great is his love, love with-out end.

Great is his love, love with-out end.

Great is his love, love with-out end.

(Hum) Great is his love, love with-out end.

(Hum) Great is his love, love with-out end.

(Hum) Great is his love, love with-out end.

6 Through the | desert his | peo-ple he | led,
   | Nations in their | great-ness he | struck,
   | Kings in their | splen-dour he |slew,

7 He let | Israel in-|he-rit their | land,
   On his | servant their | land he be-|stowed,
   He re-|membered | us in · our di-|stress,

8 He has | snatched us a-|way from our | foes,
   He gives | food to | all living | things,
   To the | God of | heav-en give | thanks,

The Grail, 1963

687

Al-le - lu - ya! Al-le - lu - ya! We will praise the name of the Lord.

Sydney Hugo Nicholson 1875–1947

Psalm 148

Alleluya! Alleluya! We will praise the name of the Lord.

1   Alleluya! *   Praise the Lord │ from the heavens,
Praise him │ in the heights.
Praise him all │ you his angels;
Praise him │ all his host.

2   Praise him │ sun and moon;
Praise him all you │ stars of light.
Praise him │ heaven · of heavens,
And you waters a-│bove the heavens.

3   Let them praise the name │ of the Lord,
For he commanded and they │ were cre-ated.
He made them fast for ev-│er and ever;
He gave them a law which shall not │ pass a-way.

Psalm 148, vv. 1–6, *Common Worship*, 2000

688

Colin Mawby b 1936

Antiphon

Al - le - - lu - ya! Al - le - - lu - ya!

Al - le - - lu - ya! Praise him with the

Psalm *Unison*

sound of trum-pets. Praise God in his ho - ly

place,_ Praise him in his migh - ty hea - vens.

Praise him for his power-ful deeds, Praise his sur-pass-ing

Antiphon

great-ness. Al - le - - lu - ya! Al - le - -

-lu - ya! Al - le - - lu - ya! Praise him with the

Psalm *Unison*

sound of trum-pets. O praise him with the

sound of trum-pet, Praise him with lute and harp.

688 Music: © The Grail

688 Words: © Set to music and reproduced by permission of The Grail, England.
Administered by A. P. Watt Ltd., 20 John Street, London. WC1N 2DR

688

Doxology

Give praise to the Fa - ther Al - migh - ty,_____ To his Son, Je - sus Christ the Lord,_____ To the Spi - rit, who dwells in our hearts,_____ Both now and for ev - er. A - men.

rit.

Slower

Antiphon

Al - le - - lu - ya! Al - le - - lu - ya! Al - le - - lu - ya! Praise him with the sound of trum - pets. __

Psalm 150

Alleluya, Alleluya, Alleluya! Praise him with the sound of trumpets.

1   Praise God in his holy place,
    Praise him in his mighty heavens.
    Praise him for his powerful deeds,
    Praise his surpassing greatness.

2   O praise him with sound of the trumpet,
    Praise him with lute and harp.
    Praise him with timbrel and dance,
    Praise him with strings and pipes.

3   O praise him with resounding cymbals,
    Praise him with clashing, with clashing of cymbals.
    Let everything that lives and that breathes
    Give praise to the Lord, Alleluya!

4   Give praise to the Father Almighty,
    To his Son, Jesus Christ the Lord,
    To the Spirit, who dwells in our hearts,
    Both now and for ever. Amen.

The Grail, 1963

689

Joseph G. Cullen b 1958

I will sing, I will sing to the Lord: glo - rious his_ tri-umph!

The Song of Moses and Miriam

I will sing, I will sing to the Lord : glorious his triumph!

1   I will sing to the Lord who has | triumph-ed gloriously,
    The horse and his rider he has thrown in-|to the sea.
    The Lord is my strength | and my song
    And has become | my sal-vation.

2   This is my God whom | I will praise,
    The God of my forebears whom I | will ex-alt.
    The Lord | is a warrior,
    The Lord | is his name.

3   Your right hand O Lord is glo-|rious in power:
    Your right hand O Lord | shatters the enemy.
    At the blast of your nostrils the | sëa · covered them;
    They sank as lead in the | migh-ty waters.

4   In your unfailing | love O Lord,
    You lead the people whom you | have re-deemed.
    And by your invin-|ci-ble strength
    You will guide them to your | ho-ly dwelling.

†5 You will bring them in and plant | them O Lord,
    In the sanctuary which your | hands · have e-stablished.

Exodus 15.1b–3, 6, 10, 13, 17,
Common Worship, Daily Prayer, 2005

690

With joy   you will draw wa - ter from the wells   of   sal - va - tion.

Anthony Gregory Murray 1905–92

† v. 4

A Song of Deliverance

With joy you will draw water from the wells of salvation.

1   'Behold, God is | my sal-vation;
    I will trust and will not | be a-fraid;
    For the Lord God is my strength | and my song,
    And has become | my sal-vation.'

2   With joy you | will draw water
    From the wells | of sal-vation.
    On that day | you will say,
    'Give thanks to the Lord * call up-|on his name;

3   'Make known his deeds a-|mong the nations,
    Proclaim that his name | is ex-alted.
    Sing God's praises who has | tri-umphed gloriously;
    Let this be known in | all the world.

†4 'Shout and sing for joy you that | dwell in Zion,
    for great in your midst is the Holy | One of Israel.'

Common Worship, Daily Prayer, 2005

691

Colin Mawby b 1936

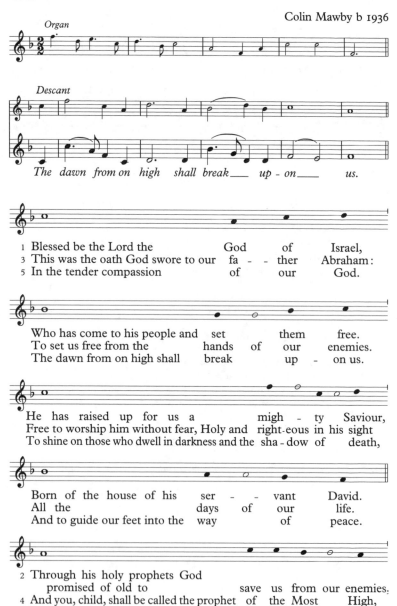

The dawn from on high shall break___ up - on___ us.

1 Blessed be the Lord the   God   of   Israel,
3 This was the oath God swore to our   fa - - ther   Abraham:
5 In the tender compassion   of   our   God.

Who has come to his people and   set   them   free.
To set us free from the   hands   of   our   enemies.
The dawn from on high shall   break   up - on us.

He   has   raised   up   for   us   a   migh - ty   Saviour,
Free to worship him without fear, Holy and   right-eous in his sight
To shine on those who dwell in darkness and the   sha - dow of   death,

Born   of   the   house   of   his   ser - - vant   David.
All   the   days   of   our   life.
And to guide our feet into the   way   of   peace.

2 Through his holy prophets God
    promised of old to   save   us   from our enemies.
4 And you, child, shall be called the prophet   of   the   Most   High,

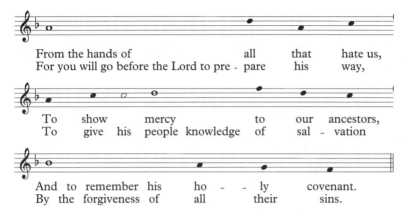

From the hands of   all   that   hate us,
For you will go before the Lord to pre - pare   his   way,

To   show   mercy   to   our   ancestors,
To   give   his   people   knowledge   of   sal - vation

And to   remember   his   ho - - ly   covenant.
By   the   forgiveness   of   all   their   sins.

Benedictus

The dawn from on high shall break upon us.

1   Blessed be the Lord the God of Israel,
    Who has come to his people and set them free.
    He has raised up for us a mighty Saviour,
    Born of the house of his servant David.

2   Through his holy prophets God promised of old to
        save us from our enemies,
    From the hands of all that hate us,
    To show mercy to our ancestors,
    And to remember his holy covenant.

3   This was the oath God swore to our father Abraham:
    To set us free from the hands of our enemies,
    Free to worship him without fear,
    Holy and righteous in his sight all the days of our life.

4   And you, child, shall be called the prophet of the Most High,
    For you will go before the Lord to prepare his way,
    To give his people knowledge of salvation
    By the forgiveness of all their sins.

5   In the tender compassion of our God
    The dawn from on high shall break upon us,
    To shine on those who dwell in darkness and the
        shadow of death,
    And to guide our feet into the way of peace.

Benedictus, Luke 1. 68–79, *Common Worship,* 2000

692

Colin Mawby b 1936

Organ

Descant

The Al-migh-ty has done great things for me: ho - ly,

ho - - ly, ho - ly_ is his name.

1 My soul proclaims the great - ness of the Lord,
3 He has mercy on those who fear him,
5 He has come to the aid of his ser - - vant Israel,

omit v. 1

(3) From generation to ge - - ne - - ration.
(5) To remember his pro - - mise of mercy,

(1) My spirit rejoices in God my Saviour;
(3) He has shown strength with his arm
(5) The promise made to our ancestors,

(1) He has looked with favour on his low - - ly servant.
(3) And has scattered the proud in their con - ceit,
(5) To Abraham and his chil - dren for ever.

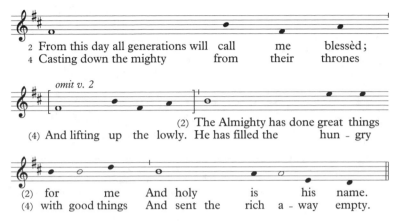

2 From this day all generations will   call   me   blessèd;
4 Casting down the mighty   from   their   thrones

omit v. 2

(2) The Almighty has done great things
(4) And lifting up   the lowly. He has filled the   hun - gry

(2) for   me   And holy   is   his   name.
(4) with good things And sent the   rich a - way   empty.

Magnificat

The Almighty has done great things for me: holy is his name.

1   My soul proclaims the greatness of the Lord,
     My spirit rejoices in God my Saviour;
     He has looked with favour on his lowly servant.

2   From this day all generations will call me blessèd;
     The Almighty has done great things for me
     And holy is his name.

3   He has mercy on those who fear him,
     From generation to generation.
     He has shown strength with his arm
     And has scattered the proud in their conceit,

4   Casting down the mighty from their thrones
     And lifting up the lowly.
     He has filled the hungry with good things
     And sent the rich away empty.

5   He has come to the aid of his servant Israel,
     To remember his promise of mercy,
     The promise made to our ancestors,
     To Abraham and his children for ever.

Magnificat, Luke 1. 46–55, *Common Worship*, 2000

693

Philip Duffy b 1943

The Lord, our God, al-migh-ty is king. Al-le-lu-

-ya. 1 Sal-va-tion and glo-ry and power be-long to our God,

Al-le-lu-ya. His judge-ments are true and just.

Al-le-lu-ya, al-le-lu-ya.

2 Praise our God, all you his ser-vants, Al-le-lu-ya.

You who fear him, small and great, Al-le-lu-ya,

al-le-lu-ya. 3 The Lord our God, the Al-migh-ty reigns,

Al-le-lu-ya. Let us re-joice and ex-ult and give him the

glo-ry. Al-le-lu-ya, al-le-lu-

-ya. 4 The mar-riage of the Lamb has come, Al-le-lu-

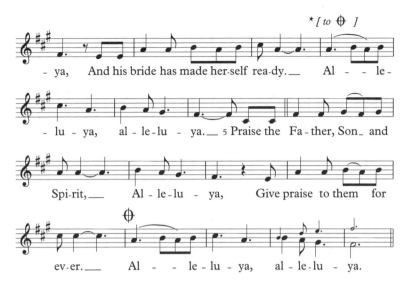

- ya, And his bride has made her-self rea-dy. — Al - - le-lu - ya, al - le-lu - ya. — 5 Praise the Fa-ther, Son_ and Spi-rit,__ Al - le-lu - ya, Give praise to them for ev-er.__ Al - - le - lu - ya, al - le-lu - ya.

* *when used at the Gradual*

Canticle of the Lamb

The Lord our God almighty, is king. Alleluya.

1 Salvation and glory and power belong to our God, Alleluya,
His judgements are true and just. Alleluya, Alleluya.

2 Praise our God, all you his servants, Alleluya,
You who fear him, small and great. Alleluya, Alleluya.

3 The Lord our God, the Almighty, reigns, Alleluya,
Let us rejoice and exult, and give him the glory. Alleluya, Alleluya.

4 The marriage of the Lamb has come, Alleluya,
And his bride has made herself ready. Alleluya, Alleluya.

5 Praise the Father, Son and Spirit, Alleluya,
Give praise to them for ever. Alleluya, Alleluya.

Revelation 19. 1–7

694

A PEOPLE'S MASS

Anthony Gregory Murray 1905–92

KYRIE

Lord,_____ have mer - cy. Lord,_____ have
mer - cy. Christ,_____ have mer - cy.
Christ,_____ have mer - cy. Lord,_____ have
mer - cy. Lord,_____ have mer - cy.

GLORIA

Unison   *Harmony*

Glo - ry to God in the high - est,_____ and peace to his
peo - ple on earth._____ Lord God, hea - ven - ly King,_____
_ al - migh - ty God and_ Fa - - ther,_____

Unison

we wor - ship you, we give you thanks, we praise you for your

Harmony

glo - - ry. Lord Je - sus Christ, on - ly

694 Music: © McCrimmon Publishing Co Ltd,
10-12 High Street, Great Wakering, Southend-on-Sea, Essex SS3 0EQ. Used by permission.

Son of the Fa - - ther, Lord God, Lamb of __
God, you take a - way the sins of the world: __ have
mer - cy on us; __ you are seat-ed at the right hand
of the __ Fa - ther: re - ceive __ our __ prayer. __
__ For you a - lone are the Ho - ly One, you a-
- lone are the Lord, you a - lone are the Most High,
Je - - sus Christ, with the __ Ho - ly Spi - rit, in the
glo - ry of God the Fa - ther. A - - - men.

694

SURSUM CORDA

Priest
The Lord be with you.
All
And al-so with you.

Priest
Lift up your hearts.
All
We lift them to the Lord.

Priest
Let us give thanks un - to the Lord our God.

All
It is right to give thanks and praise.

SANCTUS and BENEDICTUS

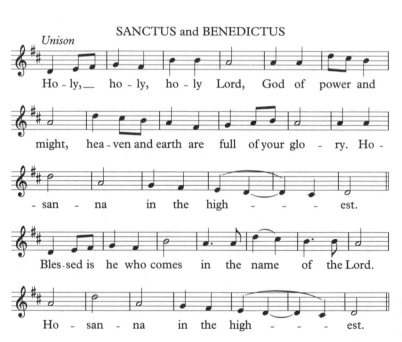

Unison

Ho - ly, ho - ly, ho - ly Lord, God of power and might, hea - ven and earth are full of your glo - ry. Ho - san - na in the high - - - est.

Bles-sed is he who comes in the name of the Lord.

Ho - san - na in the high - - - est.

ACCLAMATION

Christ has died: Christ is risen: Christ will come a - gain.

AMEN

A - - - - - men.

AGNUS DEI

Lamb of God, you take a - way the sin of the world,

have mer - cy on us. grant us peace.

Common Worship, 2000

695

ANGLICAN FOLK MASS

Martin Edward Fallas Shaw 1875–1958

KYRIE

Lord, have mer - cy up - on us, Christ, have mer -
Ky - ri - e   e - le - i - son.   Chri - - ste,

\- cy up - on us, Lord, have mer - cy up - on us.
e - le - i - son.   Ky - ri - e   e - le - i - son.

GLORIA

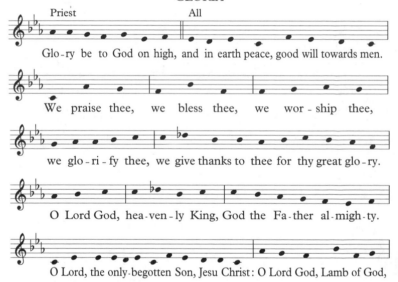

Priest   All

Glo -ry be to God on high, and in earth peace, good will towards men.

We praise thee, we bless thee, we wor - ship thee,

we glo - ri - fy thee, we give thanks to thee for thy great glo -ry.

O Lord God, hea -ven -ly King, God the Fa -ther al -migh -ty.

O Lord, the only-begotten Son, Jesu Christ: O Lord God, Lamb of God,

Son of the Fa -ther, that tak -est a -way the sins of the world,

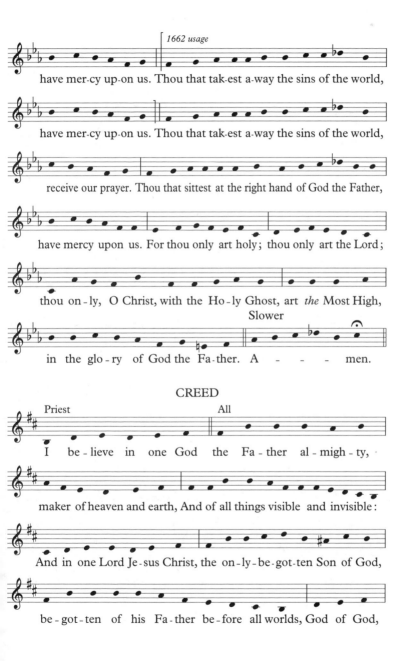

1662 usage

have mer-cy up-on us. Thou that tak-est a-way the sins of the world,

have mer-cy up-on us. Thou that tak-est a-way the sins of the world,

receive our prayer. Thou that sittest at the right hand of God the Father,

have mercy upon us. For thou only art holy; thou only art the Lord;

thou on-ly, O Christ, with the Ho-ly Ghost, art *the* Most High,

Slower

in the glo-ry of God the Fa-ther. A — — — men.

CREED

Priest   All

I be-lieve in one God the Fa-ther al-migh-ty,

maker of heaven and earth, And of all things visible and invisible:

And in one Lord Je-sus Christ, the on-ly-be-got-ten Son of God,

be-got-ten of his Fa-ther be-fore all worlds, God of God,

695

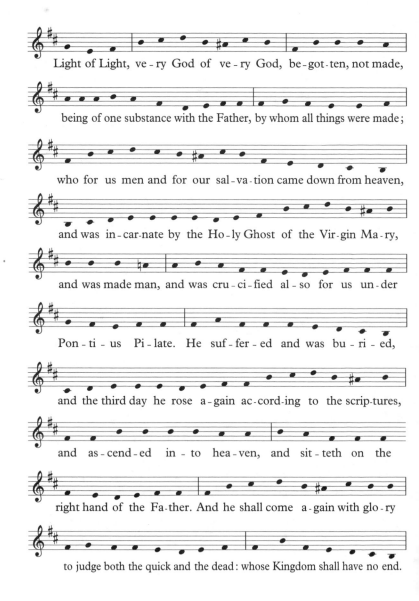

Light of Light, ve - ry God of ve - ry God, be - got - ten, not made,

being of one substance with the Father, by whom all things were made;

who for us men and for our sal - va - tion came down from heaven,

and was in - car - nate by the Ho - ly Ghost of the Vir - gin Ma - ry,

and was made man, and was cru - ci - fied al - so for us un - der

Pon - ti - us Pi - late. He suf - fer - ed and was bu - ri - ed,

and the third day he rose a - gain ac - cord - ing to the scrip - tures,

and as - cend - ed in - to hea - ven, and sit - teth on the

right hand of the Fa - ther. And he shall come a - gain with glo - ry

to judge both the quick and the dead: whose Kingdom shall have no end.

And I be-lieve in the Ho-ly Ghost, the Lord, the giv-er of life,

who pro-ceed-eth from the Fa-ther and the Son, who with the

Fa-ther and the Son to-ge-ther is wor-ship-ped and glo-ri-fied,

who spake by the pro-phets. And I be-lieve one ho-ly ca-tho-lic

and a-pos-to-lic Church. I ac-know-ledge one bap-tism for the re-

- mis-sion of sins. And I look for the re-sur-rec-tion

of the dead, and the life of the world to come. A - men.

SURSUM CORDA

Priest   All

The__ Lord be__ with__ you. And__ with thy__ spi - rit.

Priest   All

Lift_____ up your__ hearts. We lift them up un -

           Priest

- to__ the Lord.. Let us give thanks un - to__ the

695

All

Lord__ our God. It is meet and right so__ to do.__

SANCTUS

♩ = c. 69
pp

Ho - ly, ho - ly, ho - ly, Lord God of hosts,

mf

hea - ven and earth are full of thy glo - ry.

f

Glo - ry be to thee, O Lord most High. A - men.

BENEDICTUS

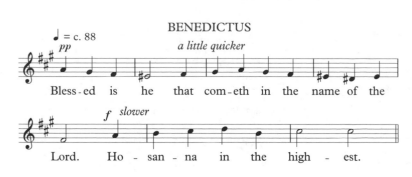

♩ = c. 88
pp   *a little quicker*

Bless - ed is he that com - eth in the name of the

f slower

Lord. Ho - san - na in the high - est.

MUSIC FOR THE EUCHARIST

1st & 2nd times

♩ = c. 69

AGNUS DEI

pp

Chanter

O Lamb of God, that tak-est a-way the sins of the world,

3rd time

Chanter

have mer-cy up-on us. O Lamb of God, that tak-est a-way the

sins of the world, grant us thy peace.

Slowly

FINAL AMEN

pp

A - - - - - - men.

A COMPOSITE MASS

KYRIE ELEISON

The six-fold *Kyrie eleison* may be sung in Greek (in harmony or in unison) to the following hymn tunes in the *New English Hymnal.*

Bread of heaven	276 (2)
Dix	47
Heathlands	366
Nicht so traurig	276 (1)
Petra	445
Ratisbon	234 (2)

In those churches where *Kyrie eleison* is sung only during penitential seasons, *Dix, Heathlands* and *Ratisbon* are suitable during Advent; *Bread of Heaven* and *Petra* during Lent; and *Nicht so traurig* during Passiontide.

In churches where it is sung throughout the year, *Bread of heaven, Petra* and *Nicht so traurig* might be used during penitential seasons, and the other tunes on other Sundays and festivals.

Care should be taken not to use a melody if the hymn with which it is associated is sung during the same service.

THE *LOURDES* GLORIA

The verses of the canticle should either be *sung* by a cantor or choir, or be *said together* by the whole congregation.

Jean-Paul Lecot

Glo - ri - a, glo - ri - a, in ex - cel - sis De - o.

Glo - ri - a, glo - ri - a, in ex - cel - sis De - o.

1 Glory to God in the high - est,
2 Lord Jesus Christ, only Son of the Fa - ther,
3 For you a - - lone are the Holy One,

and peace to his people on earth.
Lord God, Lamb of God,
you a - - lone are the Lord,

Lord God, heavenly King, almighty God and Fa - ther,
you take away the sins of the world : have mercy on us;
you alone are the Most High, Jesus Christ,

we worship you, we give you thanks, we
you are seated at the right hand of the Father: re -
with the Holy Spirit, in the glory of God the

praise you for your glo - - ry.
- ceive our prayer.
Father. A - - - - men.

696 Music: © Kevin Mayhew Ltd, Buxhall, Stowmarket, Suffolk. IP14 3BW Used by permission.

697

Franz Schubert 1797–1828
Arranged by Richard Proulx b 1937

SANCTUS and BENEDICTUS

Slowly

Ho - ly, ho - ly, ho - ly Lord, God of power and might,____ ho - ly, ho - ly, ho - ly Lord, God of power and might,____ hea - ven and earth are full,____ full____ of your glo - - ry. Ho - san - na in the high - est, ho - san - na in the high - est.

Bless-ed is he who comes____ in the name of the Lord.____ Ho - san - na in the high - est, ho - san - na in the high - est.

ACCLAMATION

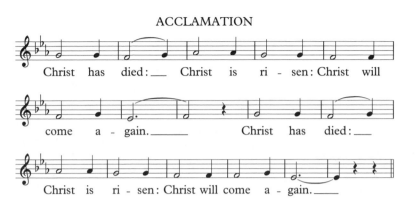

Christ has died: ___ Christ is ri - sen: Christ will come a - gain. _____ Christ has died: ___ Christ is ri - sen: Christ will come a - gain. ____

AMEN

A - - men, A - - men, A - - - men, A - men, A - - - men. _____

AN APPENDIX OF
ADDITIONAL TUNES

698

DIES DOMINICA 76 76 D   John Bacchus Dykes 1823–76

Additional tune for 311

WE pray thee, heavenly Father,
   To hear us in thy love,
And pour upon thy children
   The unction from above;
That so in love abiding,
   From all defilement free,
We may in pureness offer
   Our Eucharist to thee.

2   All that we have we offer,
   For it is all thine own,
All gifts, by thine appointment,
   In bread and cup are shown;
One thing alone we bring not,
   The wilfulness of sin,
And all we bring is nothing
   Save that which is within.

3   Within the pure oblation,
   Beneath the outward sign,
By that his operation,
   The Holy Ghost divine,
Lies hid the sacred body,
   Lies hid the precious blood,
Once slain, now ever glorious,
   Of Christ our Lord and God.

4   Wherefore, though all unworthy
   To offer sacrifice,
We pray that this our duty
   Be pleasing in thine eyes;
For praise, and thanks and worship,
   For mercy and for aid,
The catholic oblation
   Of Jesus Christ is made.

VINCENT STUCKEY STRATTON COLES 1845–1929

699

COE FEN DCM Kenneth Nicholson Naylor 1931–91

Additional tune for 373

HOW shall I sing that Majesty
    Which angels do admire?
Let dust in dust and silence lie;
    Sing, sing, ye heavenly choir.
Thousands of thousands stand around
    Thy throne, O God most high;
Ten thousand times ten thousand sound
    Thy praise; but who am I?

2   Thy brightness unto them appears,
      Whilst I thy footsteps trace;
    A sound of God comes to my ears;
      But they behold thy face:
    They sing because thou art their Sun:
      Lord, send a beam on me;
    For where heaven is but once begun,
      There alleluyas be.

3   Enlighten with faith's light my heart,
      Inflame it with love's fire;
    Then shall I sing and bear a part
      With that celestial choir.
    I shall, I fear, be dark and cold,
      With all my fire and light;
    Yet when thou dost accept their gold,
      Lord, treasure up my mite.

4   How great a being, Lord, is thine,
      Which doth all beings keep!
    Thy knowledge is the only line
      To sound so vast a deep.
    Thou art a sea without a shore,
      A sun without a sphere;
    Thy time is now and evermore,
      Thy place is everywhere.

JOHN MASON c 1645–94

700

CORVEDALE 87 87 D   Maurice Bevan 1921–2006

Additional tune for 461

Upper voices,
or full Unison mf

There's a wide - ness in God's mer - cy Like the

wide - ness of the sea; There's a kind - ness in his

jus - tice Which is more than li – ber - ty. There is

no place where earth's sor - rows Are more felt than up in

heaven: There is no place where earth's fail - ings Have such

kind-ly judge-ment given.

Harmony (preferably unaccompanied)
p

2 For the love of God is broa - der Than the

mea - sure of man's mind; And the heart of the E -

cresc.

- ter - nal Is most won-der-ful - ly kind. But we

make his love too nar - row By false li - mits of our

dim.

own; And we mag - ni - fy his strict - ness With a

zeal he will not own.

poco rit. Unison *a tempo*
f

3 There is plen - ti - ful re - demp - tion In the

blood that has been shed; There is joy for all the

Harmony
sempre f

mem - bers In the sor-rows of the head. There is

continued overleaf

700

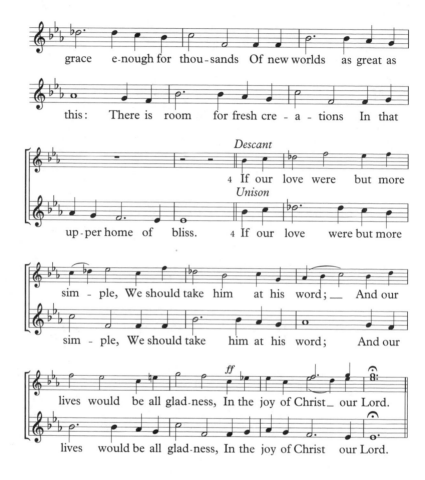

grace e-nough for thou-sands Of new worlds as great as this: There is room for fresh cre - a - tions In that

Descant
4 If our love were but more

Unison
up - per home of bliss. 4 If our love were but more

sim - ple, We should take him at his word; __ And our

sim - ple, We should take him at his word; And our

lives would be all glad-ness, In the joy of Christ __ our Lord.

lives would be all glad-ness, In the joy of Christ our Lord.

THERE'S a wideness in God's mercy,
　　Like the wideness of the sea;
There's a kindness in his justice
　　Which is more than liberty.
There is no place where earth's sorrows
　　Are more felt than up in heaven:
There is no place where earth's failings
　　Have such kindly judgement given.

2　For the love of God is broader
　　Than the measure of man's mind;
And the heart of the Eternal
　　Is most wonderfully kind.
But we make his love too narrow
　　By false limits of our own;
And we magnify his strictness
　　With a zeal he will not own.

3　There is plentiful redemption
　　In the blood that has been shed;
There is joy for all the members
　　In the sorrows of the head.
There is grace enough for thousands
　　Of new worlds as great as this:
There is room for fresh creations
　　In that upper home of bliss.

4　If our love were but more simple,
　　We should take him at his word;
And our lives would be all gladness,
　　In the joy of Christ our Lord.

FREDERICK WILLIAM FABER 1814–63

INDEXES

HYMNS SUGGESTED FOR SUNDAYS AND SOME HOLY DAYS ACCORDING TO THE *COMMON WORSHIP* LECTIONARY

In selecting the hymns an effort has been made to give variety of style, metre and key within a single service. The first list for the day provides hymns for the Eucharist in this order: Introit, before the Gospel, Offertory, Communion, Postcommunion. A Procession is suggested on major festivals, but if no procession takes place this hymn will often be more suitable than that suggested for the Introit.

The hymns usually follow the general 'feel' of the seasons and of the lessons, but for the sake of simplicity a hymn suggested by a particular lesson is still sung even in the years when that lesson is not read, provided that the link is not so strong that to sing the hymn without the reading which inspired it would appear absurd. So, for example, the Passiontide hymn *Drop, drop, slow tears* can only be sung on Proper 6 in the year that the account of the washing of Jesus' feet by the prostitute is read as the Gospel. In this case alternative hymns are suggested for the other years. Those who wish to sing hymns more explicitly related to particular lessons should consult the lists in *Sing His Glory* (Canterbury Press) but should note that that publication only lists hymns from *The New English Hymnal* which are suggested by the lectionary and thus does not explore all the hymns in the book. It is rarely, if ever, appropriate to sing four or five hymns all of which are closely related to the readings for the day regardless of other criteria mentioned above. Even the time of the year or the weather can be important factors: *Morning has broken* does not work well as the first hymn on a miserable January morning nor *Round me falls the night* at a July Evensong in broad daylight. A hymn such as *Eternal Father, strong to save* is suggested as an evening hymn at a time of year when there is a strong chance of rough seas, but the choice can only be raised as a suggestion. Those responsible for choosing the hymns must decide if it is really appropriate.

The second list of hymns, separated by an asterisk, is a mixture of those which could well be substituted for hymns in the first list and of items from which hymns could be selected for a second service such as Morning or Evening Prayer. On some Sundays it is appropriate to use both at the Eucharist and at Evensong a hymn which is particularly associated with the theme of the day – for example, *Forty days and forty nights* on Lent 1. This second list contains many general hymns unrelated to any lectionary, the use of which will enable a congregation to enjoy a large and varied selection during the course of a year.

The term *Proper* (as in Proper 6 above) is used by the *Common Worship* lectionary to describe the readings used on the Sundays between the end of the Epiphany season and the Sundays before Lent (if any) and on the Sundays after Trinity until the Fourth Sunday Before Advent. The Sundays on which these Propers are used are determined by date (Proper 6, for example, is always the Sunday between 12 and 18 June inclusive if that is after Trinity Sunday) and therefore they do not fall on the same liturgical Sunday every year. *Calendar, Lectionary and Collects* or an annual calendar will need to be consulted when using the following hymn lists in order to ascertain which Propers fall on particular Sundays in any given year.

HYMNS SUGGESTED FOR SUNDAYS
AND SOME HOLY DAYS

Numbers from 600 in these lists refer to *New English Praise*.

Advent 1 (Office Hymns 1, 2)
14 The advent of our God (or 501)
15 The Lord will come and not be slow (or 502)
16 Wake, O wake (or 9)
13 O quickly come
600 Hark what a sound (or 18)

*

449 Soldiers of Christ, arise
388 Jesus shall reign
3 Come, thou long-expected Jesus
8 Lift up your heads, ye mighty gates
18 Ye servants of the Lord
501 Drop down, ye heavens, from above
609 When rising from the bed of death

Advent 2 (Office Hymns 1, 2)
12 On Jordan's bank (or 6 or 501)
2 The heavenly word of God on high (or 8 or 502)
9 Lo, he comes (or 16 or 13)
303 O Word immortal of eternal God
500 Thy kingdom come, on bended knee

*

5 Hark, a herald voice is calling
169 Hail, harbinger of morn
170 Lo, in the wilderness a voice
315 Word of the Father
407 Lord, thy word abideth

Advent 3 (Office Hymns 1, 2)
6 Hark the glad sound (or 12 or 501)
5 Hark, a herald voice is calling (or 502)
7 Hills of the north, rejoice
275 Blessed Jesu, Mary's son
3 Come, thou long-expected Jesus

*

11 O come, O come, Emmanuel
12 On Jordan's bank
170 Lo, in the wilderness a voice
322 Pour out thy spirit from on high

443 Rejoice, the Lord is King
483 The Church of God a kingdom is

Advent 4 (Office Hymns 1, 2)
1 Creator of the stars of night (or 11 or 501)
181 For Mary, Mother of the Lord (Yr A)
or 180 Hail, O Star that pointest (Yr B)
or 166 Now in holy celebration (Yr C) (or 645 in any year)
11 O come, O come, Emmanuel (or 10)
465 Thou didst leave thy throne and thy kingly crown
17 When came in flesh the incarnate word

*

4 Gabriel's message does away
5 Hark! a herald voice is calling
8 Lift up your heads, ye mighty gates
9 Lo! he comes with clouds descending
286 From glory to glory advancing
501 Drop down, ye heavens, from above
602 Born in the night
645 The breath of God

Christmas Midnight Mass (Procession 30, 33 or 34)
41 Where is this stupendous stranger (or 38 or 21)
42 While shepherds watched (or 505)
32 O little town of Bethlehem
28 In the bleak mid-winter (or 30 or 35)
26 Hark! the herald-angels sing

*

29 It came upon the midnight clear
31 O little one sweet
19 Come, thou redeemer of the earth (esp as Introit or Procession)

23 Behold, the great Creator makes
470 To the name of our salvation
55 Hail to the Lord's anointed

Epiphany 2 (Office Hymns 53, 54)
53 This day, the first of days
57 The race that long in darkness pined
55 Hail to the Lord's anointed (Yrs A & B)
or 56 Songs of thankfulness and praise (Yr C)
302 O thou, who at thy Eucharist didst pray (in Unity Week) otherwise 41
393 Lead us, heavenly Father, lead us

*

200 Jesus calls us! o'er the tumult (Yr B)
216 Disposer supreme (Yr B)
390 Jesus, where'er thy people meet
420 O Jesus, I have promised
422 O Lord of heaven, and earth, and sea
365 God moves in a mysterious way
366 God of mercy, God of grace
623 I come with joy to meet my Lord (in Unity Week)
647 Will you come and follow me (Yr B)

Epiphany 3 (Office Hymns 53, 54)
451 Songs of praise the angels sang
366 God of mercy, God of grace
353 Dear Lord and Father (Yr A)
or 56 Songs of thankfulness and praise (Yr B)
or 55 Hail to the Lord's anointed (Yr C)
41 Where is this stupendous stranger (or 302 in Unity Week)
483 The Church of God a kingdom is
649 How shall they hear the word of God

*

200 Jesus calls us! o'er the tumult (Yr A)
298 May the grace of Christ our Saviour

284 Father, we thank thee who hast planted
425 O love how deep, how broad, how high
360 Firmly I believe, and truly
361 Forth in the peace of Christ we go
623 I come with joy to meet my Lord (in Unity Week)
647 Will you come and follow me (Yr A)

Epiphany 4 (Office Hymns 53, 54)
426 O praise the Lord, ye servants of the Lord (or 644)
206 Christ is our corner-stone (or 341 in Yr A – see Proper 3)
56 Songs of thankfulness and praise (Yr A)
or 430 O thou, not made with hands (Yrs B & C)
or 157 Hail to the Lord who comes (Yr C)
299 My spirit longs for thee
362 Glorious things of thee are spoken

*

44 Faithful vigil ended
52 O worship the Lord in the beauty of holiness
209 Lo! God is here, let us adore
257 This is the day the Lord has made
249 Round me falls the night
314 With solemn faith we offer up

Proper 1 (Office Hymns 53, 54)
254 Come, let us with our Lord arise
324 Thine arm, O Lord, in days of old (Yrs A & B)
or 343 Bright the vision that delighted (Yr C)
433 O worship the King
464 Thou art the way
235 Forth in thy name, O Lord, I go

*

347 Come, gracious Spirit, heavenly Dove
340 Beyond all mortal praise
339 Be thou my vision
495 God is working his purpose out
369 Happy are they, they that love God

67 Forty days and forty nights
70 Lord Jesus, think on me
74 O for a heart to praise my God

*

61 O Christ, who art the light and day
62 Ah, holy Jesu, how hast thou offended
75 O thou, who dost accord us
382 Jesu, grant me this, I pray
84 It is a thing most wonderful
63 All ye who seek a comfort sure
606 Enter our hearts, O holy Lord

Lent 1 (Office Hymns 59, 60)
63 All ye who seek a comfort sure (or 507)
67 Forty days and forty nights
68 Jesus, Lord of life and glory
83 Glory be to Jesus
64 Be thou my guardian and my guide

*

65 Christian, dost thou see them
299 My spirit longs for thee
333 All my hope on God is founded
445 Rock of ages! cleft for me
507 Hear us, O Lord, have mercy upon us
607 With joy and by the Spirit led

Lent 2 (Office Hymns 59, 60)
66 Forgive our sins as we forgive (or 507)
73 My God, I love thee, not because (or 642)
76 Take up thy cross the Saviour said
62 Ah, holy Jesu, how hast thou offended
450 Soldiers, who are Christ's below

*

72 My faith looks up to thee
350 Come, O thou traveller unknown
449 Soldiers of Christ, arise
453 Stand up! stand up for Jesus
382 Jesu, grant me this, I pray
337 As pants the hart for cooling streams

Lent 3 (Office Hymns 59, 60)
60 O kind Creator, bow thine ear (or 507)
414 O for a closer walk with God (or 607 in Yr A)
65 Christian, dost thou see them
69 Lord, in this thy mercy's day (or 72)
379 In the cross of Christ I glory

*

81 Dost thou truly seek renown
71 Maker of earth, to thee alone
374 How sweet the name of Jesus sounds
474 Who is this, so weak and helpless
376 I heard the voice of Jesus say
628 And didst thou travel light

Lent 4 (Office Hymns 59, 60)
77 The God of love my shepherd is
369 Happy are they, they that love God
75 O thou, who dost accord us
300 O food of men wayfaring
383 Jesu, lover of my soul (or 387)

*

282 Faithful shepherd, feed me
457 The King of love my shepherd is
458 The Lord my pasture shall prepare
85 Jesu meek and lowly
434 Oft in danger, oft in woe
61 O Christ, who art the light and day

Lent 5 (Office Hymns 78, 79)
91 Sweet the moments, rich in blessing (or 79)
82 Drop, drop slow tears (or 92)
90 O sacred head, sore wounded
85 Jesu, meek and lowly
95 When I survey the wondrous Cross

*

62 Ah, holy Jesu, how hast thou offended
78 Sing, my tongue, the glorious battle
80 Servant of God, remember
84 It is a thing most wonderful
92 There is a green hill far away

Easter Day (Office Hymns 100, 101)
(Procession 109;
Evening Procession 125)
110 Jesus Christ is risen today
111 Jesus Christ is risen! (or 519)
104 At the Lamb's high feast we sing
(or 106)
123 Walking in a garden (or 122)
120 Thine be the glory

*

102 A brighter dawn is breaking
115 Now the green blade riseth
117 The day of resurrection!
125 Ye sons and daughters of the King
119 The strife is o'er, the battle done
113 Love's redeeming work is done
610 Finished the strife of battle now

Easter 2 (Office Hymns 100,101)
106 Come, ye faithful, raise the strain
117 The day of resurrection! (or 519)
116 O praise our great and glorious
Lord (or 101)
125 Ye sons and daughters of the King
(or 276 or 633)
105 Christ the Lord is risen again

*

100 The day draws on with golden
light
107 Good Christian men, rejoice and
sing
108 Hail Easter bright, in glory dight
112 Jesus lives! thy terrors now
118 The Lord is risen indeed!
121 This joyful Eastertide! away with
sin and sorrow

Easter 3 (Office Hymns 100, 101)
124 Ye choirs of new Jerusalem
114 Now is eternal life
103 Alleluya! Alleluya! hearts to heaven
and voices raise (or 400 in Yr A)
121 This joyful Eastertide! away with
sin and sorrow
113 Love's redeeming work is done

*

112 Jesus lives! thy terrors now
317 With Christ we share a mystic
grave

363 Glory in the highest to the God of
heaven
375 I danced in the morning when the
world was begun
345 Christ is the King! O friends,
rejoice
279 Come, risen Lord, and deign to
be our guest
280 Deck thyself, my soul, with
gladness
633 Come, my way
637 Hark my soul! it is the Lord
(esp Yr C)

Easter 4 (Office Hymns 100, 101)
100 The day draws on with golden
light (or 101 or 108)
118 The Lord is risen indeed!
122 Thou hallowed chosen morn of
praise
282 Faithful shepherd, feed me
119 The strife is o'er, the battle done
(or 120)

*

105 Christ the Lord is risen again
114 Now is eternal life
446 Rejoice! the Lord is King
457 The King of Love my shepherd is
458 The Lord my pasture shall prepare
459 The Lord's my shepherd, I'll not
want
400 Light of the minds that know him
638 In heavenly love abiding

Easter 5 (Office Hymns 100, 101)
107 Good Christian men, rejoice and
sing
111 Jesus Christ is risen!
296 Lord, enthroned in heavenly
splendour
102 A brighter dawn is breaking
(or 308)
437 Praise the Lord! ye heavens adore
him

*

374 How sweet the name of Jesus
sounds
376 I heard the voice of Jesus say
347 Come gracious Spirit, heavenly
Dove

301 O most merciful! O most
    bountiful!
410 We hail thy presence glorious
                  *
240 When all the world to life is
    waking
416 O God of Bethel, by whose hand
287 Glory, love, and praise, and
    honour
332 All hail the power of Jesu's name
328 God be in my head
442 Prayer is the soul's sincere desire
245 God, that madest earth and
    heaven

Proper 12 (Office Hymns 149, 150)
336 Angel-voices, ever singing
482 Spread, O spread the mighty
    word (Yr A)
  or 277 Bread of the world, in mercy
    broken (Yr B)
  or 406 Lord, teach us how to pray
    aright (Yr C)
338 At the name of Jesus (or 271)
307 Sweet Sacrament divine
361 Forth in the peace of Christ we go
                  *
276 Bread of heaven, on thee we feed
354 Eternal Father, strong to save
397 Let us, with a gladsome mind
423 O Lord of hosts, all heaven
    possessing
  64 Be thou my guardian and my
    guide
350 Come, O thou traveller unknown
357 Father, hear the prayer we offer
698 We pray thee heavenly father
    (also 311)

Proper 13 (Office Hymns 149, 150)
234 Christ, whose glory fills the skies
    (or 618)
419 O Holy Spirit, Lord of grace
381 Jerusalem the golden
309 Victim divine, thy grace we claim
368 Guide me, O thou great
    Redeemer
                  *

345 Christ is the King! O friends,
    rejoice
279 Come, risen Lord, and deign to
    be our guest
333 All my hope on God is founded
364 God is love; let heaven adore him
478 Ye watchers and ye holy ones
392 Lead, kindly light, amid the
    encircling gloom
455 Strong Son of God, immortal
    Love

Proper 14 (Office Hymns 149, 150)
430 O thou not made with hands
335 All praise to thee, for thou, O
    King divine (or 649 in Yr A)
470 To the name that brings salvation
313 Wherefore, O Father, we thy
    humble servants
443 Rejoice! the Lord is King
                  *
438 Praise to God, whose word was
    spoken
331 Abide with me, fast falls the
    eventide
412 My soul, there is a country
513 God is love, and where true love is
400 Light of the minds that know thee
699 How shall I sing that majesty
    (also 373)
454 Still throned in heaven, to men in
    unbelief
647 O God beyond all praising

Proper 15 (Office Hymns 149, 150)
446 Sing Alleluya forth in duteous
    praise
357 Father, hear the prayer we offer
273 And now, O Father, mindful of
    the love
279 Come, risen Lord, and deign to
    be our guest
427 O praise ye the Lord! Praise him
    in the height
                  *
149 Father, we praise thee, now the
    night is over
  63 All ye who seek a comfort sure

614 Hail redeemer, king divine
629 Be still, for the presence of the
     Lord

Candlemas (Office Hymn 156)
  (Ceremony 506 or 657;
  Procession 33) No Introit
156 Sing how the age-long promise
     of a Saviour
157 Hail to the Lord who comes
187 Virgin-born, we bow before thee
247 O gladsome light, O grace
     (Evening)
  or 234 Christ, whose glory fills the
     skies (Morning)
                    *
 44 Faithful vigil ended
338 At the name of Jesus

The Blessed Virgin Mary
  (Office Hymns 180, 181)
  (Procession 188)
183 O glorious Maid, exalted far
182 Her Virgin eyes saw God incarnate
     born
185 Sing we of the blessèd Mother
     (or 188)
187 Virgin-born, we bow before thee
186 Tell out, my soul, the greatness of
     the Lord (or 185)
                    *
180 Hail, O Star that pointest
181 The Lord whom earth and sea and
     sky
184 Shall we not love thee, Mother
     dear
188 Ye who own the faith of Jesus
161 For Mary, Mother of the Lord
187 Virgin-born, we bow before thee
289 Hail, true Body, born of Mary
478 Ye watchers and ye holy ones
601 A maiden most gentle
645 The breath of God

Apostles (Office Hymns 213, 214)
  (Procession 197)
  Proper Hymn of the Saint
  (except St Peter &
  St Paul, and St Thomas)

213 The eternal gifts of Christ the
     King (or 214)
216 Disposer supreme (or 226)
     (or 171 for St Peter & St Paul
     or 173 for St Thomas)
225 Give me the wings of faith
230 Palms of glory, raiment bright

Dedication Festival (Office Hymn 204)
  (Procession 210)
209 Lo! God is here, let us adore
206 Christ is our corner-stone
     (or 522)
205 Christ is made the sure
     foundation
208 In our day of thanksgiving one
     psalm let us offer
413 Now thank we all our God
                    *
204 Blessed City, heavenly Salem
207 Eternal Power, whose high abode
211 O Word of God above
479 Faith of our fathers, taught of old
483 The Church of God a kingdom is
441 Pray that Jerusalem may have
471 We love the place, O God
444 Rejoice today with one accord

All Saints (Office Hymn 196)
  (Procession 197)
224 For all thy saints, O Lord (or 196)
230 Palms of glory, raiment bright
     (or 523)
231 Who are these, like stars
     appearing
227 How bright these glorious spirits
     shine!
198 The Church triumphant in thy
     love
                    *
225 Give me the wings of faith to rise
226 Hark! the sound of holy voices
229 Joy and triumph everlasting
381 Jerusalem the golden
472 When all thy mercies, O my God
432 O what their joy and their glory
     must be

TABLE OF SUGGESTED PSALMS
FOR USE AT THE EUCHARIST

It has not been possible to provide the proper psalm for every Sunday and Festival in the *Common Worship* Lectionary. Nevertheless, the selection of psalms included in the *New English Hymnal* (528 to 540) and *New English Praise* (668 to 692) normally makes provision for at least one Sunday in the three-year cycle for most of the year, using the 'related readings cycle' proposed by the lectionary. In suggesting alternatives where exact provision has not been made, we have either selected the same psalm for the other years in the cycle, or chosen from the psalms proposed for use at other services on the same Sunday. In some cases we have had to substitute another suitable psalm, but use of the following table should ensure that a wide selection of psalms will be sung during the course of the year.

Proper psalms are printed in normal type, and suggested alternatives in *italic type*. Numbers below 600 refer to the *New English Hymnal*, and those from 600 to *New English Praise*.

Day	A (or all)	B	C
Advent 1	*528*	678	528
Advent 2	677	*528*	691
Advent 3	692	685 or 692	690
Advent 4	678	692	692 or 678
Christmas	535		
Christmas 1	687		
Christmas 2	*535*		
Epiphany	677		
Baptism of Christ	671		
Candlemas	535		
Sundays between Epiphany and 2 before Lent	*535 (before Candlemas),* *672, 680,* *682, 683*	683 (Epiphany 4) 672 (Proper 2)	
2 before Lent	686	537	675 or 676
1 before Lent	*681*	*681*	681
Ash Wednesday	532 or 658		
Lent 1	*679*	528	679
Lent 2	684	*684*	*684*
Lent 3	*533*	*533*	533
Lent 4	670	*670*	*670*
Lent 5	*685*	532	685
Palm Sunday	673		
Maundy Thursday	538		
Good Friday	*673*		
Easter Day	539		
Easter 2	*688*	*688*	539 or 688

Day	A (or all)	B	C
Easter 3	538	*538*	672
Easter 4	670	670	670
Easter 5	673	*687*	687
Easter 6	*535*	535	*535*
Ascension Day	531 or 680		
Easter 7	*531 or 680*		
Pentecost	537		
Trinity Sunday	668	671	668
Corpus Christi	538		
Proper 4	673	*529*	*673*
Proper 5	*529*	*674*	672
Proper 6	682	*530*	*538*
Proper 7	*534*	*534*	*676*
Proper 8	*530*	672	*684*
Proper 9	540	*684*	*672*
Proper 10	676	*675*	528
Proper 11	*682*	670	669
Proper 12	*679*	540	*533*
Proper 13	540	*533*	679
Proper 14	*533*	*679*	529
Proper 15	*683*	*683*	*678*
Proper 16	*685*	*536*	536
Proper 17	*669*	669	*685*
Proper 18	*668*	*528*	*668*
Proper 19	536	538	532
Proper 20	540	*529*	*534*
Proper 21	528	*531*	*531*
Proper 22	678	668	*681*
Proper 23	670	*681*	683
Proper 24	*681*	679	684
Proper 25	*531*	685	534
4 before Advent	530	*530*	*530*
3 before Advent	679 or 686	*686*	686
2 before Advent	*535*	*535*	535
Christ the King	*680*	680	*680*
All Saints	*688*		
Dedication	*534*		
Harvest	675	685	682
Blessed Virgin Mary	674		
Apostles	*538*		

INDEX OF PSALMS AND CANTICLES

The following is a list of psalms and canticles which appear in *The New English Hymnal* and *New English Praise*. It will be useful for those wishing to find versions of psalms appointed by any lectionary. Responsorial psalms are listed first, followed by psalms as hymns (metrical psalms) or plainsong chants. Numbers below 600 refer to the *New English Hymnal*, those from 600 to *New English Praise*.

Psalm	Hymn(s)	Psalm	Hymn(s)
Ps 5	236	Ps 98	535
Ps 8	668	Ps 99	681
Ps 15	669	Ps 100	682, 334
Ps 22	515	Ps 103	536, 436
Ps 23	670, 77, 457, 458, 459	Ps 104	537, 433, 518
Ps 25	528	Ps 111	683
Ps 29	671	Ps 116	538
Ps 30	672	Ps 118	539
Ps 31	673	Ps 121	684
Ps 33	529	Ps 122	441
Ps 34	467	Ps 126	685
Ps 42	337	Ps 136	686, 397
Ps 42–3	530, 518	Ps 145	540
Ps 45	674	Ps 148	687, 437
Ps 47	531	Ps 150	680
Ps 51	532, 657, 658		
Ps 63	533		
Ps 65	675, 676		
Ps 67	366		
Ps 72	677		
Ps 80	678		
Ps 84	534		
Ps 85/6	15		
Ps 90	417		
Ps 91	679		
Ps 93	680, 266		

Canticle	Hymn(s)
Benedicite (short form)	656
Benedictus	691
Magnificat	692, 186, 652
Nunc Dimittis	506, 656, 44
Isaiah 12	690, 518
Song of Deliverance	690
Song of the Red Sea	518
Song of Moses and Miriam	689
Canticle of the Lamb	693

ALPHABETICAL INDEX OF TUNES

METRICAL INDEX OF TUNES

INDEX OF COMPOSERS, ARRANGERS,
AND SOURCES OF TUNES

INDEX OF AUTHORS, TRANSLATORS,
AND SOURCES OF WORDS

INDEX OF FIRST LINES AND TUNES